KU-033-527

Patsy Westcott

rheumatism and arthritis

Recipes and Advice to Stop the Pain

food solutions

TED SMART

rheumatism and arthritis

Recipes and Advice to Stop the Pain

Executive Editor – Jane McIntosh
Editor – Katey Day
Art Director – Keith Martin
Executive Art Editor – Geoff Fennell
Book Design – Birgit Eggers
Picture Research – Rosie Garai and
          Christine Juneman
Production – Lucy Woodhead

First published in Great Britain in
2000 by Hamlyn, a division of
Octopus Publishing Group Limited,
2–4 Heron Quays, London E14 4JP

Copyright © Octopus Publishing
Group Limited 2000
ISBN 1 85613 717 1
Reprinted in 2002

This edition produced for
The Book People Ltd,
Hall Wood Avenue,
Haydock,
St Helens WA11 9UL

A catalogue record for this book is
available from the British Library

Printed in China

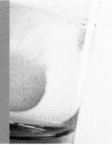

contents

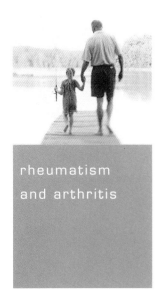

rheumatism
and arthritis

Arthritis and rheumatism affect over eight million people living in the UK today and account for one in five visits to the doctor's surgery. In the USA it's estimated that one in seven Americans suffer from these complaints. There are over 200 different kinds of arthritic and rheumatic conditions and they can affect anyone of any age, wherever they live. Although sometimes their effects are mild, many people suffer for years with pain, swelling, fatigue and increasing immobility. This book is about how you can help yourself if you have arthritis or rheumatism, especially by paying attention to what you eat.

Traditional and non-conventional medicines have always maintained a connection between arthritis and rheumatism and food, and over the years a whole host of different diets and foods have been suggested as cures but until fairly recently most orthodox doctors have dismissed the idea of food as a treatment. Scientific medicine held sway and the idea that there was 'a pill for every ill' prevented doctors and scientists looking beyond the laboratory for medical treatments. However, in the past few years, this has begun to change. Some of the impetus has come from large-scale studies looking at which groups of people are most susceptible to developing particular diseases. Many of these studies, which were carried out over a long period of time, had quite striking results. To take heart disease as an example, experts found that people living in Mediterranean countries were far less likely to die of heart disease than people living in northern Europe and north America. The inescapable conclusion was that something in the diet and lifestyle of people in these countries helped protect their hearts and blood vessels. It was the same story when scientists turned their attention to cancer. Women living in Japan and China, for instance, were found to be at a far lower risk of breast cancer. As interest in diet began to increase, numerous research studies were carried out into the effects of diet on a whole host of illnesses and conditions. Gradually it came to be recognized that a diet rich in fruit and vegetables actively helped protect against ageing and degenerative conditions such as diabetes, heart disease, cataracts and, yes, arthritis. In fact in the past few years an enormous body of research has been done that proves beyond a shadow of a doubt that the way we live our lives and the food we eat and drink plays an important part in helping us to stay strong and healthy and in preventing disease. Time and again nutrients and chemicals found in foods such as fruit and vegetables have been found to protect the body and even halt the onset of disease in its tracks. Even if someone has already succumbed to an illness a healthy diet can help boost the immune system and provide the body with the ammunition it needs to fight back.

While this research has been going on, other researchers have been examining the role that food intolerances and allergies may play in triggering many 20th-century diseases. Joint and muscular aches and pains are often symptoms of sensitivity to a particular food. At the same time many arthritic diseases involve an inflammatory reaction, which is essentially an immune reaction. Could it be that for some people the trigger that sets off this reaction is food? If anything, orthodox doctors were even more sceptical about this idea than they were about the idea that food can protect against disease. However, a few pioneering doctors persevered and now there is growing evidence that sensitivity to various common foods can play a part in certain kinds of arthritis for some people and that eliminating these foods can bring a relief of symptoms. These discoveries have provided new hope for sufferers.

In this book you will learn what foods you can eat to enhance your immune system and improve the function of your joints and muscles. You will also learn how to find out if something you are eating might be contributing to your arthritis or rheumatism. And to help you put all you have learnt into practice, there are over sixty delicious recipes designed to help you to feel healthier and fitter and free from pain.

One of the worst aspects of a chronic illness is the way it makes you feel you are not in control. It can seem as if your body has let you down and that doctors and medical staff are the ones in charge of your life. One way to increase your well-being is to regain your sense of being in the driving seat. As what you eat is such a fundamental part of your life, learning about the best diet to help you stay strong is important. Knowing as much as possible about your condition is also vital. As well as the advice on food and recipes, you will find information about how the joints, muscles, bones and tendons work and how arthritic and rheumatic conditions affect them, together with advice on ways in which you can help yourself. You will also find out about orthodox and complementary treatments, including the drugs and surgery used to treat arthritis and rheumatism and safe, non-drug therapies that will ease the pain.

RIGHT: Aromatherapy has been shown to help reduce stress and can alleviate pain and stiffness in some people's joints.

RIGHT: Tomatoes and other members of the solanaceae family, such as potatoes and aubergines, are thought to be factors in triggering arthritis in some sufferers.

Arthritis and rheumatism are chronic conditions. That means that by their very nature they go on for some time. There's no guarantee of a cure and you may always need to have medical treatment but by the time you have finished reading this book you should have some solutions.

chapter 1

You only have to watch a flamenco dancer, a yogi or a tennis player in action to appreciate the many different ways in which our bodies can move. **To understand what goes wrong in arthritis and rheumatism you need to know a bit about the joints, muscles, bones and ligaments** that together make up the body's musculo-skeletal system.

This system is a masterpiece of structural engineering constructed around the skeleton, which consists of some 206 bones. These are connected to each other at the joints which are held in place by ligaments and moved by means of the contraction and relaxation of the surrounding muscles. There are many different joints in the body, some fixed, some with restricted movement and others highly mobile.

Each joint is constructed in a different way and **by understanding the exact cause of your pain, whether it is the bones themselves, the cartilage or the membranes around the joint, you will know what steps to take to control it** for a happier, healthier life.

the joints and the musculo-skeletal system

BELOW: The hand is made up of many separate bones and joints, making it particularly vulnerable to arthritic problems.

BOTTOM: The symphysis pubis is a cartilaginous joint with only slight movement, whereas the synovial ball and socket joints at the hips allow a wide range of movements.

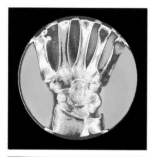

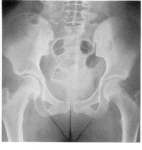

what are joints?

A joint is the junction where two bones meet. They have two purposes: to hold our skeletons together, and to allow us to move. Although most of us think of movement as the most important function of joints, in fact their role in keeping parts of our body in place is equally important. The rigid joints of the skull, for instance, are vital to protect the delicate soft tissue of our brains. Although by their very nature joints are the most vulnerable parts of our skeleton they are constructed in such a way as to maintain their stability and help them resist injury. Strong muscles can help support and protect the joints making them less likely to be accidentally injured.

types of joint

Although there are many different types of joints, experts tend to classify them in two main ways: first by what they do – that is how much movement they allow – and second by what they are made of, their structure. In terms of what they do, there are three different kinds of joint:

Fixed joints with no movement, like the bones of the skull. Slightly moveable joints, like the vertebral joints in our backs. Mobile joints that are highly moveable like those in our legs and arms.

how joints work

How joints work depends to a large extent on the way in which the bones within the joint are united. In some, known as fibrous joints, the bones are linked by tough fibrous tissue which allows virtually no movement. Fibrous joints include those in the skull, in which the cranial bones are spliced by short tough fibres that harness the bones firmly together, so protecting the brain from blows and jolts.

In other joints, known as cartilaginous joints, the ends of the bones are linked by the tough connective tissue known as cartilage, or gristle. These sorts of joints may be fixed or slightly moveable. An example of a cartilaginous joint is the symphysis pubis joint in the pelvis. Normally fairly rigid, it is able to open slightly, enabling the bones to move so as to accommodate the growing baby during pregnancy and birth. In fact during labour the bones can separate by as much as 1.5 cm ($^3/_4$ inch).

In a third type of joint, called the synovial joint, the bones are separated by a fluid-filled cavity, which allows the joint to make a wide range of movement. The term synovial comes from the slippery membrane that lines the joint cavity, known as the synovium. All the joints of the limbs and many other joints in the body come into this category. Inside synovial joints a coating of smooth cartilage covers the ends of the bones. This acts as a shock-absorbing cushion, preventing the bone ends from being crushed and helping the joint to move smoothly. The joint cavity is filled with a liquid which is rather like egg white, called synovial fluid, which nourishes and lubricates the joint allowing it to move smoothly and preventing wear and tear. The cavity is surrounded by a strong, fibrous capsule called the joint capsule, which holds the joint in place and prevents excessive movement. This is lined with a layer of loose connective tissue called the synovial membrane.

The strength and stability of synovial joints is aided by ligaments made of strong elastic material that join the two bones within the joint, helping keep them in place and controlling their movement. Muscle tendons, strong fibrous cords made of a protein called collagen, also add stability. These tendons are attached to the bone and also to the muscles and kept taut by the tone of the muscles. Well-toned muscles in the shoulders and the knees for example will help keep the joints stable and prevent injury. The joint capsule and the ligaments are well supplied with nerves that send messages to the brain about the position of the joints and help to maintain muscle tone. Movement is controlled by muscles that are attached to the bones by tendons, which do not stretch, and by ligaments. Without ligaments to hold them in place the bones would be extremely unstable and liable to dislocate when we move.

how our bodies move

Our movements depend on the interaction between joints, muscles, tendons and ligaments. Muscles are attached to bones or to connective tissue at either end. When we tighten a muscle across the joint – either deliberately or involuntarily – the muscle pulls on the bone at its end causing it to move, a bit like a piece of elastic pulling on a stick. The muscles at the joints work in groups, with some tightening and others relaxing the joint, enabling our bodies to move in many different ways. Ligaments work with the muscles to stabilize the joints and prevent the muscles from moving the bones outside their range of movement. The range of movement of which we are each capable varies tremendously and depends to a large extent on the flexibility of the joints. For instance, dancers and sports people often have a wide range of joint movement. The good news is that even if your joint movement is limited because of rheumatism or arthritis it is usually possible to increase it by exercising.

The simplest joint movement is a gliding movement that happens when one flattish bone surface glides or slides over another similar surface. Gliding joints are found in the wrists and in some of the bones in

BELOW: Exercise can help to increase joint movement and suppleness, which is particularly valuable in rheumatism and arthritis sufferers.

the feet. Angular movements occur when the angle between two bones changes, for example when you nod your head or bend backwards or forwards from the waist. Rotating movements occur when the bone revolves around its own axis, for example if you circle your shoulders or your hips like a belly dancer.

types of synovial joint

There are many different kinds of synovial joint. In plane joints the surfaces of the bones within the joint are flat allowing sliding or gliding movement. In hinge joints the ends of the bones are convex or concave so that one bone fits into the other. These joints are found at the elbow, the knee and the fingers and allow them to bend and straighten, just like a hinge.

Pivot joints, found in the elbow and the back of the neck between the first and second vertebrae, in which the rounded end of one bone fits into

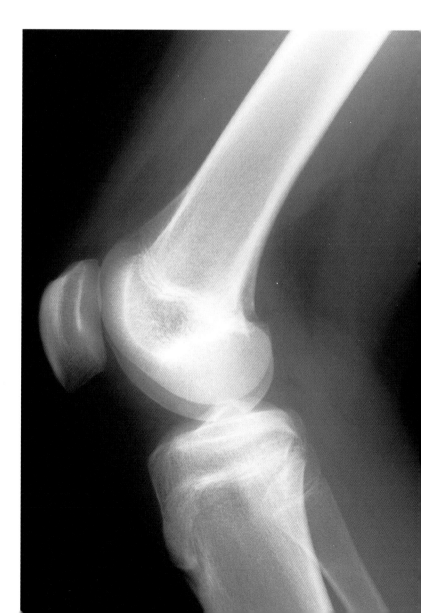

RIGHT: The knee is a synovial hinge joint, in which one bone fits into the other, allowing the knee to open and close like a hinge.

a ring of bone and ligaments, allow rotating movements. For example, the pivot joint in the back of the neck enables us to shake our heads, while the pivot joint in the elbow lets us rotate the lower arm, so we can twist a doorknob. The joints which allow the widest movement of all are the ball and socket joints, such as those found at the hip and the shoulder. In this kind of joint, the ball-shaped end of one bone fits into a socket-shaped cavity, permitting a wide range of movement, backwards, forwards, sideways or in rotation.

Joints can be exceedingly complex in structure. The knee joint, for example, is three joints in one. It is constructed to enable the bones of the leg to extend, flex or rotate, letting us sit, walk, run, dance, swim and perform a whole range of different activities. It is strengthened and supported by muscles and tendons and is capable of withstanding a force of seven times the body weight. If you watch a weight-lifter doing squats you can see this in practice. However, because it is so complex, the knee joint is vulnerable to injury during sport or exercise.

what can go wrong?

There are some 200 different disorders affecting the bones, muscles, ligaments and joints of the musculo-skeletal system. Some are caused by injury or wear and tear, others by the effects of different diseases. They include diseases such as rheumatoid arthritis (RA); gout, caused by inflammation of the joint lining; osteoarthritis, degeneration the cause of which is unknown; soft tissue problems causing pain in the soft tissues around the joints, such as tennis elbow and fibromyalgia; and backache.

In the next chapter we will examine some of the most common rheumatic and arthritic problems and what causes them in more detail.

TOP: Swimming would be impossible without the complex knee joints which, as well as a simple hinge action, allow the lower leg to rotate, flex and extend.

ABOVE: When problems occur with the joints, exercising them is vital to improve their mobility and reduce pain, and eventually build up the muscles to help protect the joints in the future.

chapter 2

The word rheumatism is a rather unscientific term which is usually used by lay people to describe aches and pains and stiffness in the joints and muscles. The term arthritis on the other hand is used more precisely by doctors to describe disease or damage to the joints from one of a number of different causes.

Many attacks of rheumatism are acute, that is they come on suddenly and go away in time, often without any treatment. This applies especially to backache and soft tissue problems. Arthritis, however, is frequently more troublesome. **Although the term arthritis is used as if it were just one condition, in fact there are a multitude of different types**.

Arthritis can affect just one joint or many, and can vary in its effects from mild aching and stiffness to severe pain and disability. Many types of arthritis are chronic diseases, that is, they never go away completely, although there may be periods when they flare up followed by periods of remission.

types of arthritis

ABOVE: Although osteoarthritis usually strikes after middle age, some young people can be affected too.

secondary and occupational arthritis

Secondary osteoarthritis may develop many years after an injury to a joint or as a result of repeated minor injuries to a joint. This may be due to performing a repetitive activity in the course of work or leisure. Babies who were born with a dislocated hip (clicky hip) sometimes develop secondary arthritis later in life. Occupational arthritis is a type of secondary arthritis that can develop in people whose work involves excessive use or stress on certain joints. Inhaled chemicals such as silica dust may push up the risk of developing rheumatoid arthritis by causing an immune reaction.

osteoarthritis

Osteoarthritis (OA), which you may also hear called osteoarthrosis, is the most common type of chronic arthritis. It mainly affects people from middle age onwards, although sometimes it can afflict younger people. The condition is found more in women than men and the first symptoms are often experienced around the time of the menopause.

In the past osteoarthritis was thought to be a result of wear and tear on the joints over time. Recently thinking has changed because osteoarthritis does not appear to be any more common in people whose joints are subject to a lot of wear and tear, such as athletes, than it is in others. Experts now think that OA is linked to the normal ageing process and that practically all of us would develop it if we were to live long enough.

The changes in the joints are often so mild that they are barely noticeable, although for some people the condition gets progressively worse over a period of time. The sites most often affected are the hands, knees, hips, feet and spine, especially the joints at the neck and in the lower back. Symptoms include early morning stiffness that wears off with activity. Where inflammation is present the joint may become swollen, tender and warm. However unlike rheumatoid arthritis the person does not feel unwell. In the later stages affected joints may make a crunching noise, known as crepitus, when they move caused by the eroded surfaces of the joint rubbing together.

HOW OA DEVELOPS

Osteoarthritis usually develops slowly over a number of years. It causes thinning of the smooth articular cartilage that coats the ends of the bones within a joint. You will remember from the previous chapter that it is this material that prevents bones from rubbing against each other and helps the joints to work smoothly. What happens is that the normal process of breakdown and repair that takes place in the cartilage is accelerated so that cartilage breaks down more quickly than it is replaced. It is not known exactly why this happens, although it may be particularly likely if a joint has to work hard and there is stress on the cartilage, but when it does occur, the cartilage becomes roughened, frayed and eroded.

Over time the bone beneath the cartilage thickens and broadens. Bony spurs known as osteophytes form at the outer end of the joint, causing a knobbly appearance, and the synovial membrane and joint capsule thicken and the joint space narrows. When this happens the ligaments around the joint capsule become looser making it difficult for the ligaments to perform their job of holding the joint in position and preventing excessive movement. This leaves the joint more prone to damage and this in turn exacerbates cartilage loss.

Although OA, unlike rheumatoid arthritis, is not primarily an inflammatory disease there may be inflammation, triggered by fragments of bone and cartilage breaking off and irritating the synovial membrane. However unlike rheumatoid arthritis, in OA the inflammation is mild and is caused by the disease rather than the other way round.

rheumatoid arthritis

Rheumatoid arthritis (RA) is one of the most common types of arthritis, affecting some one in three people in the UK. The disease usually starts between the ages of 30 and 50, although it can come on at virtually any stage from childhood to old age, and it affects more women than men. Often the disease develops slowly, although in about one in five of those affected by RA the onset is sudden, and in about one in twenty the disease becomes progressively worse quite quickly. For most people the disease progresses in fits and starts with flare-ups when symptoms become marked and periods when the disease is quiet.

HOW RA DEVELOPS

In the early stages you may notice that some joints, most commonly those in the fingers, knuckles and wrists, feel tender, warm, red and stiff, especially first thing in the morning, making it difficult to get up and get on with your daily routine. As the disease progresses there may be increasing pain and disability as cartilage and bone within the joints become damaged. The effect of the disease on the joints varies a lot, with some people sustaining little or no damage and others experiencing such severe damage that the appearance of the affected joints is

ABOVE: One of the main symptoms of osteoarthritis is stiffness early in the morning, making getting up and starting the day a real challenge for sufferers.

distorted and deformed. The most commonly affected joints are the shoulders, wrists, knuckles and middle joints of the fingers, the knees, ankles and middle joints of the toes. Eventually arthritis may spread to the elbows, shoulders, hips, ankles and occasionally even the jaw. A classic characteristic of the disease is that it affects the joints symmetrically, so for example if your right ankle is swollen and tender your left ankle will be too. As well as the physical symptoms of tenderness, redness and swelling, people with RA often experience extreme fatigue, depression and irritability.

HOW IS RA CAUSED?

The precise causes of RA are still unknown. Until recently it was considered to be an auto-immune disease, one in which the body's normal defence mechanism, the immune system, which is designed to protect it from invaders, turns its weapons against the body, in this case the tissues of the joints, causing damage to the cartilage that covers the

osteoporosis

If you have rheumatoid arthritis or another inflammatory arthritic condition you are more at risk of developing osteoporosis, the disease in which the bones become thin and brittle and prone to break. The disease occurs when the natural process of bone build-up and bone loss is accelerated, so that more bone is lost than is gained. Women are more at risk of osteoporosis, especially at the menopause, partly because they have lighter, more fragile bones and partly because of dwindling levels of the female sex hormone, oestrogen, which helps to protect against bone loss. Lack of weight-bearing activities increases the risk as do smoking and drinking. Steroid drugs, sometimes used to treat rheumatoid and other types of inflammatory arthritis, also increase the risk.

Treatment may be by hormone replacement or other drugs which act directly to prevent bone loss. However prevention is better than cure: making sure you get plenty of weight-bearing exercise – anything that slightly stresses the bones such as walking, running or weight-lifting. Eating calcium-rich foods, giving up smoking and not drinking too much can also help.

ABOVE: Smoking increases the risk of osteoporosis and women nearing the menopause, who are most at risk, should consider giving up the habit.

bone ends and sometimes the bones, ligaments and tendons as well. The presence of an antibody, known as the rheumatoid factor, which can be detected by a blood test in some people with RA, seemed to support this idea. It is now believed that the process may be rather more complicated. For a start the rheumatoid factor is not always present when the disease first strikes, as you would expect it to be. What is more, even in people with severe symptoms of the disease the rheumatoid factor is not always present for a long time. The one thing that is certain is that in RA the immune system goes into overdrive.

It is not known exactly what causes the immune system to become so frenzied, although in a small number of people with RA the disease runs in the family. Some doctors and scientists suspect that an infection may spark the immune system into action. However, despite a great deal of research, no single infectious agent has yet been identified.

EFFECTS OF RA

Whatever the cause, the overactivity of the immune system has a number of different effects. First, the synovial membrane that lines the joint becomes inflamed causing synovial fluid to accumulate in the joint cavity. Blood rushes to the area carrying inflammatory blood cells and this makes the joint swell, redden and feel warm. The build-up of fluid and inflammatory blood cells within the joint capsule stretches it, causing stiffness and pain. At the same time, chemicals released as a result of the inflammatory reaction irritate nerve endings and this too causes pain.

Not surprisingly all this pain can make the person feel extremely debilitated, especially during flare-ups when the inflammatory process is active. There may also be other symptoms of immune overactivity, such as weight loss, lack of energy and swollen glands. In some people other parts of the body such as the lungs and the blood vessels may become inflamed as well. If the disease progresses, the inflamed synovial membrane thickens and forms a piece of abnormal tissue called a pannus (Latin for rag), which clings to the cartilage. In time the continuing production of inflammatory cells erodes the cartilage, and sometimes the bone beneath it as well, and scar tissue forms at the bone ends. Eventually the scar tissue ossifies (turns into bone) and the bone ends fuse together. It is this ankylosis (Greek for stiffness) which leads to the bent, deformed fingers seen in people with severe RA. Of course, not everyone with RA has the disease as severely as this.

episodic arthritis

In episodic arthritis, as the term suggests, the person has repeated episodes of inflammatory arthritic symptoms such as pain, swelling, reddening and stiffness. As with RA, symptoms are due to inflammation of the synovial membrane and excess production of synovial fluid, but in episodic arthritis the disease stops at the initial stage and does not go on to attack the cartilage and bone as it does in RA. However, about one in three people with episodic arthritis go on to develop RA. Episodic arthritis is sometimes known by the old-fashioned term palindromic rheumatism.

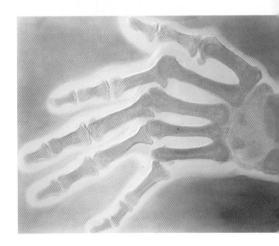

ABOVE: In extreme rheumatoid arthritis, the continued inflammatory reaction results in ossification of the scar tissue, leading to fused, immobile joints with bony growths.

ABOVE: Gout usually affects the joint at the base of the big toe, but other joints are at risk. They become inflamed and swollen, as in other arthritic diseases, making diagnosis hard.

gout

Gout, caused by a build-up of uric acid crystals in a joint, is much more common in men than women, because male biochemistry leads them to produce more uric acid than women. Women who develop the condition often do so at the menopause as a result of hormonal changes which result in raised blood levels of uric acid.

The onset of an attack of gout is often sudden and dramatic, with a rapid build-up of excruciating pain, often in the joints at the base of the big toes, although other joints such as those in the ankles, knees, hands, wrists or elbows may also be affected. The joint aches and becomes swollen and painful. An attack normally settles over a period of days or weeks as the joint returns to normal.

Many people only ever have a single attack of gout, however others are plagued by repeated attacks. Untreated gout can be a crippling disease which attacks and damages other joints and can make the bone ends fuse, leading to deformities and disabilities. Fortunately with today's drug treatments this rarely happens any more. Diagnosis may sometimes be difficult as the condition can be mistaken for other arthritic conditions such as rheumatoid or osteoarthritis, especially when an attack affects more than one joint.

WHAT HAPPENS IN GOUT?

Gout is caused by an over-reaction of the immune system triggered by a build-up of uric acid crystals in a joint, most often the joint at the base of the big toe. Uric acid is a natural waste product found in the blood, normally passed out of the body in the urine. However if blood levels of uric acid rise too high the blood becomes saturated, and crystals of urate form in the blood and the synovial fluid that bathes the joints. These crystals are deposited in the cartilage where they set up a vicious circle of inflammation, swelling and pain. When urate crystals form in a joint the body's immune system sends a type of white blood cell, called a neutrophil, to the area in an attempt to rid it of the crystals. These blood cells ingest the crystals which burst the membranes of the neutrophils unleashing a torrent of inflammatory enzymes together with lactic acid which causes the synovial fluid to become more acidic. The acidity of the fluid causes more crystals to form, while the damage to the neutrophils causes them to send messages for reinforcements to the immune system – and so it goes on. It is vital that gout is treated promptly to break this vicious circle. Taking a stoic approach and trying to grin and bear the symptoms can cause an attack to escalate, making it much more difficult to treat.

Uric acid is produced when the body breaks down other chemicals called purines, some of which are derived from DNA, the genetic material in our cells, as well as from foods and drinks such as liver and red wine (hence gout's traditional although unfair association with eating and drinking to excess). It is not known why some people produce more uric acid than others, although men have higher levels in their blood than women, and obese people produce more purines. Some people, it seems, are predisposed to produce excessive amounts of uric acid, while others flush the chemical out of their body slowly. In addition, there are some people with a fault in their metabolism that causes them to produce too much purine, while some drugs, such as aspirin and diuretics (water tablets) used to treat high blood pressure, prevent uric acid from being removed from the blood stream effectively.

ABOVE: Gout is caused by high levels of uric acid in the body, which derive from many sources, including red wine.

ankylosing spondylitis

Ankylosing spondylitis, AS (the term comes from ankylosing meaning stiffness and spondylitis meaning inflammation of the spine) is one of a group of conditions known as spondyloarthropathies. Others in the group include psoriatic arthritis (which is associated with the skin complaint psoriasis), arthritis linked to inflammatory bowel diseases such as Crohn's disease and ulcerative colitis) and reactive arthritis (see right). It is a type of inflammatory arthritis which mainly affects the joints of the spine, especially the sacroiliac joints at its base, causing stiffness and lower back pain. If the disease is left untreated bony spurs grow out from both sides of the vertebrae and fuse them together causing rigidity and irreversible loss of movement. The spine may also become bent. Fortunately this can be prevented by staying active, keeping the spine mobile and taking anti-inflammatory drugs prescribed by the doctor. The condition affects three times more men than women, although it may affect more women than previously thought, as milder forms may be misdiagnosed as backache.

HOW IS IT CAUSED?

It is not known exactly what causes AS but research suggests some important clues. AS tends to run in families and it has been found that nine out of ten people with the condition belong to a white blood cell group called HLA-B27. Scientists discovered that people who possess HLA-B27 are particularly susceptible to developing reactive arthritis

reactive arthritis

Reactive arthritis is arthritis (pain and stiffness in the joints) following a bacterial, viral or other infection elsewhere in the body. It is not known exactly what causes the joint symptoms, however they may continue for many years after the initial infection has settled. Mumps, infectious hepatitis, glandular fever, chicken pox and HIV are among the viruses known to spark reactive arthritis. Reiter's syndrome is another type of reactive arthritis. It often follows a urinary tract infection (UTI) or bowel infection and affects the eyes and urinary tract as well as the joints.

ABOVE: AS causes pain and stiffness in the lower back, down the backs of the legs and in the leg joints. This is most marked in the mornings or after a period of inactivity.

fibromyalgia and ME
(myalgic encephalomyelitis)

ME (chronic fatigue syndrome), is sometimes associated with fibromyalgia. In ME joint pain is just one of a range of symptoms, the most pronounced of which is an overwhelming sense of tiredness. The experts are still arguing about the cause of ME. Because it sometimes appears to follow a viral or bacterial infection such as glandular fever or gastroenteritis it is sometimes called post viral fatigue syndrome. Some doctors maintain that the symptoms are related to psychological rather than physical problems.

(arthritis that develops following an infection). People with AS have high levels of antibodies to a certain infective agent, a type of bacteria known as Klebsiella. This inhabits the guts and the lungs of about 5 per cent of us quite naturally and does not cause any symptoms. It has been found, however, that people with AS have high levels of antibodies to Klebsiella, a sign that their immune system is reacting to the bacterium. It has also been discovered that Klebsiella produces a protein which is chemically similar to HLA-B27. It has been suggested that this similarity may spark off an immune reaction that leads to AS. Although there is still much work to be done to unravel the precise connection between Klebsiella and AS, the research offers some promising new avenues to explore.

EFFECTS OF AS

The first symptoms are stiffness and pain in the lower back, which are often mistaken for ordinary backache or lumbago. There may be pain in the buttocks, down the back of the thighs as well as in the lower back. Symptoms tend to be much worse in the early morning or after a period of sitting down but improve with activity. Sometimes the symptoms appear first in the hips, knees or ankles. While some people with AS experience little more than a few mild aches and pains, others have more troublesome symptoms, such as chest pain, caused by inflammation of the joints between the ribs and the breastbone, loss of appetite and fatigue. In about a quarter of people with AS, inflammation may also affect the eyes causing a pink, painful eye, and cause digestive disturbances. The disease can also lead to osteoporosis of the spine.

After some months the lower back may stiffen, sometimes painlessly. In some people the disease burns itself out at this stage and causes no further problems but in others further attacks of pain and stiffness recur over a period of years. When the inflammatory activity ceases, no further attacks occur, although there will continue to be stiffness of the spine and the chest, if affected.

The effects of the disease vary from person to person and will depend on how long the disease has continued and how strong the inflammatory activity has been during this time. Most people with AS are able to live normal lives, despite some pain and stiffness. However those who have the disease more severely will experience greater restrictions. A great deal can be done to prevent many of the more disabling effects, which is why it is vital to get the disease diagnosed at an early stage.

rheumatic problems

FIBROMYALGIA

Fibromyalgia, which in the past was described as fibrositis or muscular rheumatism, is an extremely common type of rheumatism in which widespread aches and pains affect the muscles and ligaments. The condition tends to affect more women than men, especially in youth and middle age, and may last for months or even years. Symptoms can range in severity from barely interfering with everyday life to being so painful and disabling that they cause serious disruption to work, rest and play.

HOW IS FIBROMYALGIA CAUSED?

The exact causes of fibromyalgia are unknown although some research suggests it is a result of lack of deep sleep. When we sleep we go through alternate cycles of deep sleep and lighter REM (rapid eye movement) or dreaming sleep. Researchers have found that in people with fibromyalgia the part of the cycle of deep sleep is constantly interrupted by REM sleep. Intriguingly, in experiments, healthy people who are deliberately woken up during deep sleep develop the tender nodules and other symptoms of fibromyalgia. The initial sleep disturbance may be sparked by an emotional crisis, difficulties at home and work, disease or pain, creating a vicious circle of sleep disturbance, followed by pain and tenderness leading to further sleep disturbance.

EFFECTS OF FIBROMYALGIA

The areas most often affected are around the shoulders and the neck although tender nodules or lumpy areas can often be felt in the soft tissue in other places such as the elbows, buttocks, hips and above the knees. These feel excruciatingly sore and are tender when pressed. Although most of us feel some discomfort when these areas are pressed, in fibromyalgia the points are tender at a pressure which would not normally produce pain. The pain is experienced as aching, stiffness and tiredness in the muscles and in the tendons and ligaments around the joints and it may be worse early in the morning or with activity.

People with fibromyalgia often suffer from feelings of overwhelming fatigue and insomnia, frequently accompanied by lack of energy, muscular fatigue (aching muscles on minor exertion) and lack of staying power,

polymyalgia rheumatica

This is a rare condition causing inflammation of the muscles of the neck, shoulders, upper arms, buttocks and thighs. It mainly affects people over 50. It comes on suddenly, with severe morning stiffness in these areas which eases as the day goes on but often returns in the evening. There may be lack of appetite and loss of weight. The joints are not usually affected, although in some people there may be inflammation in the shoulder, hip and wrist joints. Rarely, but seriously, the arteries in the neck and head (cranial arteritis) may be affected causing headaches and in rare instances a risk of blindness. Treatment, which is with steroid tablets that usually lead to dramatic relief within a day or two, is usually needed for between one and three years, during which time the dose is gradually reduced.

BELOW: Fibromyalgia is thought to be connected to a lack of deep sleep.

tendonitis and tenosynovitis

Tendonitis is inflammation of the tendons, the strong, inelastic fibrous cords that join muscles to bones or to each other. The condition may follow injury. Tendons are surrounded by a tendon sheath, the inner lining of which, like the joints, is composed of synovial membrane. Inflammation of this lining is called tenosynovitis. It usually affects the tendons in the hands and wrists, often as a result of overuse. People working in jobs which involve constant use of the hands and wrists, for example keyboard workers, are prone to the condition.

ABOVE: Overuse of the hand and wrist tendons and joints can result in tendonitis, tenosynovitis and arthralgia. Keyboard work is a typical cause.

BELOW: Fibromyalgia results in tender joints, making everyday activities, like climbing stairs, painful for sufferers.

psoriatic arthritis

This is a type of arthritis that affects people with the skin condition psoriasis. In psoriasis, the skin cells are produced too quickly causing layers of cells to accumulate, forming thickened patches covered with dead, flaking scales. It is not known exactly what causes psoriasis, but it is thought to be an immune disorder.

Any joint can be affected by psoriatic arthritis although those at the tips of the fingers, the knees and the spine are most often involved. The condition usually sets in between the ages of 30 and 50 and affects men and women equally.

making it difficult to cope with everyday activities like walking upstairs, doing the housework and going shopping, which most people manage without a thought.

A range of symptoms affecting other parts of the body are sometimes associated with fibromyalgia. These include tingling, numbness, poor circulation, swollen hands and feet, headaches, forgetfulness, irritability, depression, urgency of urination (feeling an extreme urge to pass urine) and irritable bowel syndrome with symptoms alternating between diarrhoea, constipation and bloating. Because these symptoms may be linked to other illnesses it is important to get a proper medical diagnosis.

BURSITIS

A bursa is a protective fluid-filled pad situated near a joint, where a tendon or muscle crosses bone or other muscles. We have about 150 bursae in sites such as the elbows, shoulders and knees; they are made of balls of fibrous tissue lined with synovial membrane which produces fluid. Bursitis is inflammation of a bursa, causing the production of excess fluid which leads to pain and swelling. Housemaid's knee (prepatellar bursitis) and student's elbow (olecranon bursitis) are both types of bursitis caused by pressure, friction or mild injury of the synovial membrane: in the former by prolonged kneeling and in the latter by prolonged pressure of the elbow on a desk. Subdeltoid bursitis, which affects the shoulder, can lead to a frozen shoulder, in which the shoulder becomes stiff and painful and movement is restricted. Bursitis is also a feature of rheumatoid arthritis.

NON-ARTHRITIC JOINT PAIN (ARTHRALGIA)

Some people experience pain in the joints that is not associated with inflammation. This non-arthritic joint pain (sometimes known as arthralgia) can be caused by overuse. People who use a keyboard a lot in their work can develop arthralgia in the hands and wrists and professional footballers may develop it in their knees. Non-arthritic joint pain is also a feature of food intolerance and allergy. In this case there are often other symptoms such as headaches, bowel disturbances, fatigue and a general feeling of being unwell.

lupus (systemic lupus erythematosus, SLE)

This is a chronic auto-immune disorder in which the immune system turns against the connective tissue causing inflammation. The disease affects the skin, the joints and the kidneys. Symptoms include a red, blotchy rash on the cheeks and the bridge of the nose, joint pains, fever, fatigue, loss of appetite, nausea, weight loss and a general feeling of being unwell. Left untreated, some people with SLE risk developing anaemia, kidney damage, inflammation of the lining of the lungs (pleurisy) and even inflammation of the membrane surrounding the heart (pericarditis). The abnormal immune response can be triggered by sunlight and certain drugs. In the past SLE could be life threatening. However, with the anti-inflammatory and the immunosuppressive drugs available today, it can be effectively treated.

arthritis and
rheumatism –
what are they?

when to consult the doctor

We all experience the odd aches and pains or twinges in our muscles and joints from time to time, especially if we've taken part in some unaccustomed activity. Usually if you think about it you can track the discomfort back to something like going swimming when you haven't been for a while, joining a gym or exercise class or heaving furniture around when rearranging a room or moving house. These aches and pains are caused by the build-up of lactic acid in the muscles, a waste product produced by the body when we exercise, and they fade over the course of a few days. As your body gets used to the activity in question you are less likely to ache when you do it. The kinds of aches and pains to be suspicious of are those which cannot be traced back to any obvious cause, and which persist or even get worse.

If you experience any of the following, they could be a sign that you are developing a rheumatic disease so it would be a good idea to make an appointment to see your doctor:

Persistent pain or stiffness in a joint or soft tissue that is not connected with some unusual activity or exercise.
Pain associated with stiffness or difficulty moving a joint.
Swelling or inflammation of a joint accompanied by redness or throbbing.
Joint pains related to other symptoms, such as extreme fatigue that isn't linked to late nights or overwork, weight loss, night sweats, skin rashes, mouth ulcers and a general feeling of being below par.

getting a diagnosis

If you have symptoms that suggest arthritis or rheumatism it is vital to get a diagnosis so that the appropriate treatment can be prescribed by your doctor, and to help you determine ways in which you can help yourself. Bear in mind that it can sometimes be difficult to reach a definite diagnosis in the early stages of an arthritic or rheumatic illness as the symptoms may be vague at first and only become more specific as the disease progresses. Sometimes you may even be given one diagnosis only to be told later that you have a different condition.

A consultation with a doctor usually has three distinct elements, which help him or her make a diagnosis: a medical history, a physical examination and tests. If you turn out to have one of the potentially more serious rheumatic conditions or if the doctor is having trouble reaching a diagnosis he or she is likely to refer you to a specialist rheumatologist, a consultant with detailed knowledge and experience of dealing with arthritis and rheumatism.

your medical history

In the first part of a visit to your doctor he or she will usually take your medical history. The doctor will want to know details of your symptoms, so be prepared to answer questions about what they are, when they occur and if there are any circumstances in which they are worse or better. Usually the doctor will ask some other questions to help him or her pin down your symptoms more specifically. These may include questions about other recent medical problems you may have had, such as rashes and skin problems, bowel problems, urinary tract infections, sore throats, conjunctivitis, sexually transmitted diseases and sleep disturbance, which may be linked to conditions causing joint or muscle pain. He or she may also ask you about your lifestyle, including your diet, your job and leisure activities, to see if these offer any clues as to why you might have developed this particular condition at this time.

the physical examination

The doctor will examine you, concentrating on the areas in which you have described symptoms and paying particular attention to any pain and tenderness, any swellings or deformities or signs of inflammation in the joints or soft tissue. He or she may take your temperature to check for any signs of a fever. In some cases the consultation will stop there and the doctor will offer a diagnosis. However if he or she suspects a rheumatic disease further tests may be done to help define more exactly the condition affecting you.

tests for arthritis

Medical tests are designed to determine what condition is affecting you and to rule out any other causes for your symptoms. Once a diagnosis has been reached other tests may be done to help the doctor predict how your condition might progress and to try to decide on the most appropriate treatment. The tests shown in the chart on the next page are some of those used to detect arthritic and rheumatic conditions. They may look daunting when you see them listed all together in this way. Bear in mind that you are unlikely to have all of them.

ABOVE: Make an appointment to see your doctor if you have on-going aches and pains that cannot be explained by your recent activities. You may well receive a diagnosis straight away, but do not be alarmed if you are sent for tests to pinpoint the exact cause of your condition.

TEST	WHAT IT IS	WHY IT IS DONE
Anti-nuclear antibodies	A blood test	To check for types of antibodies present in the blood in certain types of arthritis and connective tissue disorders such as lupus and scleroderma.
Arthrography	A type of X-ray in which a dye is injected into the joint	To view specific damage to a joint.
Arthroscopy	A small telescope is used to examine the joint, usually under general anaesthetic	To inspect the inside of a joint, such as the knee, where damage would not be visible on an X-ray
Biochemical profile	A blood test	To examine chemicals in the blood which indicate kidney and liver function and to check for salt and calcium levels – all of which can be affected by arthritis or its treatment
Biopsy	A small piece of tissue is taken and examined under a microscope	To help diagnose certain types of arthritis
Blood count	A blood test	To check for anaemia by counting the numbers of red and white blood cells. Arthritis can cause lowered blood counts as can certain drugs used to treat the disease
Erythrocyte sedimentation rate	A blood test	To discover how quickly blood cells settle in a test tube. This reflects the amount of inflammation being caused by arthritis

TEST	WHAT IT IS	WHY IT IS DONE
HLA-B27 test	A blood test	To aid diagnosis of spondylitis, reactive and psoriatic arthritis
Urate	A blood test	To check for urate levels in order to diagnose gout
Urine test	A sample of urine is analysed for certain substances	To help diagnosis and check certain drug treatments
X-ray	Radiation is passed through certain parts of the body to produce a picture of the bones and joints	To help ascertain what changes arthritis may be causing
Computerized tomograph (CT)	A type of scan in which a computer is used to analyse X-ray images of the body	To view the areas affected by arthritis
Dual emission X-ray	A type of X-ray	To check for bone density in absorptiometry suspected (DEXA) osteoporosis
Isotope bone scan	A type of X-ray in which a radioactive marker is injected into the blood	To show areas of inflamed bone
Magnetic resonance imaging (MRI)	A type of scan in which radio waves are used to create an image of soft tissues such as cartilage tendons and nerves	To check for inflammation especially in the spine and the knee
Synovial fluid analysis	A sample of synovial fluid is taken from a joint using a syringe	To check for infections or gout

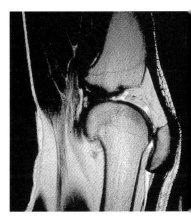

ABOVE: A scan of a healthy knee joint seen from the side. The bones are shown in blue and the other internal tissues are shown in orange.

Most of us feel the need to look at the way we live from time to time and to assess whether we are doing what we really want to do and **getting the most out of life**. Many people take the opportunity to take a good look at themselves and their lifestyle at a particular time such as the new year or a significant birthday. A major change such as being diagnosed with a chronic illness can also provide you with the impetus to examine how you live and to think whether there are any ways in which you can **change your life to make it easier** or more satisfying.

If you've just been diagnosed with an arthritic or rheumatic disease, you may be feeling anxious about what the future might hold and how it is likely to affect you and those around you but there may also be a sense of relief, especially if it has taken some time to reach a definitive diagnosis. Now at last something can be done and you can **apply yourself to the task of working out how you can best help yourself**.

helping
yourself

dealing with fatigue

As we saw in the last chapter, many conditions affecting the joints and muscles have fatigue as one of their main symptoms. This can make the symptoms more difficult to deal with, as things always seem worse when we are tired.

Learning how to adapt your lifestyle will help you feel a greater sense of control and help minimize fatigue. As you learn to live with your illness you will discover that some things take it out of you more than others, for example travelling or going to a party, and learn to plan your life to allow yourself time to recover. Once you've developed a feel for how things are likely to affect you, you will begin to feel you have more control over your life. You will learn to identify the times when you will feel more tired and the times when are likely to have more energy and plan activities around them. Of course there may be times when you are completely thrown and some seemingly minor activity leaves you feeling utterly wiped out. When this happens the best course is usually to accept the way you are feeling and give yourself time to recover and feel more energetic.

Tiredness itself can lead to feelings of depression and despair. Learning how to minimize stress and think more positively, and avoiding undue tiredness will help you to cope better. However, if you remain constantly depressed do not be afraid to seek professional help.

learning to prioritize

Putting first things first is essential in avoiding undue stress and helping you to make the most of your energy. It can help to keep a diary for a week or so and write down in detail how you spend your time, noting particular activities, how long they took and how you felt afterwards. You can then use what you have discovered to think about how to plan your life so that you make the best use of your time and energy. You may need to accept that there are some occasions when you feel so lacking in energy that the best thing to do is simply to give in to the feeling. However there may be other times when a change of activity, a distraction or doing some exercise or stretches help you to feel more energetic.

BELOW: Many people find that being diagnosed with a chronic illness leads them to really think about their. Maybe changes to accommodate your illness will enable you to cope with it much better

making compromises

You are going to have to compromise in some ways. The point to bear in mind is that having a chronic illness does mean change and that can be difficult to accept. Stress is often a result of feeling helpless and unable to cope. Learning how to transform feelings of helplessness by thinking positively and making practical changes will help you feel less stressed.

One way to enhance your feeling of control is to get as much information as you can about your condition. Organisations such as Arthritis Care and the Arthritis Research Campaign have useful leaflets and a wealth of information that can help you learn more about your illness and ways of coping with it.

maintaining social contact

Feelings of isolation can be a real problem when you have a chronic illness, especially if there are times when you are housebound. We all need the support of others from time to time and not just when we are feeling miserable. It is vital for our sense of self to have others with whom we can share the good times as well as the bad. Maintaining contact with your friends and family and arranging visits and activities you can do together will help you feel more positive and less isolated.

Sometimes interesting things happen when a major change takes place in your life. Some of your friends or family may turn out to be a real support; others may be less so. In fact it's a common observation that you learn who your friends are when you go through a crisis or change of any kind.

It is quite common to find there are people among your friends who find it more difficult to deal with your illness than others. This can be difficult to accept. However, when you think about it, each of us has our own strengths and weaknesses – and this applies to our friends and acquaintances as well. The trick is to learn how to relate to each other so that you complement one another and benefit from the way you interact in positive ways. For example, the friend who feels uncomfortable talking about your illness may be wonderful at arranging some pleasant distracting activity that you both enjoy.

You may want to share the experience of your illness with others who have the same condition. Arthritis Care has support groups and runs a course, Challenging Arthritis, where you can learn positive ways of thinking and dealing with the condition from one another. Not everyone wants to join a group, however. Some people feel that being with others in the same situation makes them focus too much on their illness when they would rather forget about it as much as possible and concentrate on getting on with life.

how the world sees you

You may notice that other people view you differently if you are slower to do things or visibly disabled. You may feel that people ignore you or don't take you seriously. Unfortunately that may also apply to some medical staff you encounter too. Public transport and buildings like cinemas

TOP: Many sufferers learn to predict the changes in their energy levels, allowing them to schedule the activities they enjoy for a time when they will feel good.

ABOVE: Social relationships may change after your diagnosis; some friends will react better than others, but nearly all will adjust in time.

helping
yourself

and theatres may seem designed to exclude you. Not surprisingly this can make you feel angry – it can seem as if the whole world is conspiring to treat you as a second-class citizen.

On a practical note, life is getting easier in many ways for disabled people now that disabled groups are making their voices heard and public awareness increases. However you may still need to develop your assertion skills to help you deal with people who view you as an inferior citizen just because you have some difficulties in doing certain things.

dealing with practical problems

It's a harsh fact that some types of arthritis can make the everyday tasks and activities that most healthy people take for granted more difficult to manage. It can be stressful and frustrating to discover that things like turning on a tap, opening a bottle or going up and down steps are no longer the simple business they once were, especially if you have always been independent.

Adopting a positive approach to your difficulties and trying to view them as a challenge will help you to regain a sense of control. No one is pretending that it is always easy to adapt to the changes that arthritis and rheumatism may bring and there are bound to be days when you feel angry and miserable, especially during flare-ups. However as time goes on and you learn to live with your condition, you may even find that taking life at a slightly slower pace enables you to appreciate it more and get more out of it. Often we are so busy rushing from one thing to the next that we never get time to savour the moment.

special equipment

Fortunately there are a multitude of practical gadgets on the market, and adaptations that can be made to your household appliances that can help you to do everyday tasks in a fraction of the time, if you are having difficulties. For example, if your hands are affected by arthritis you might consider having your taps fitted with a lever that you can turn on and off by pushing with your wrist rather than twisting the tap head. Other gadgets can help you to open cans, bottles and jars, cut vegetables, slice bread, pour tea, squeeze toothpaste, switch on the lights, and so on. The list is almost endless.

If you are having difficulty changing gears when you drive you might, if you can afford it, consider getting an automatic car, and if manoeuvring the steering wheel is difficult then getting a car with power steering can

BELOW: Even everyday activities can at times seem too difficult, but developing a positive approach, by viewing each problem as a challenge, can greatly help.

help. It is vital to keep driving, if you can, as this will enable you to remain independent. Research has shown that feeling a sense of control and autonomy is important in keeping depression at bay.

You can get information about ways in which you can adapt your life from the occupational therapist at the hospital, self-help groups like Arthritis Care, disabled living centres or advice lines such as Disablement Information and Advice Line (DIAL). Your local social services department can help you if live alone or need advice on services such as home help or care. You can get advice on work through the Employment Services Disability Service Teams.

exercise and relaxation

Getting a balance between activity and rest is especially important when you have arthritis or rheumatism. It may be tempting not to exercise because of fear of or actual pain when you move. However stiff joints that are difficult to move become even more painful and immobile without exercise, while lack of activity can increase feelings of worthlessness and depression. Gentle, regular exercise on the other hand can help improve flexibility, reduce pain, improve bone density and, by strengthening the muscles that support the joints, help to protect them.

Exercise has other benefits too. Research studies have shown that exercising helps to lift anxiety, depression and anger and improves mood, concentration and self-esteem – both in the short and the long term. Exercising also helps distract you from worries and anxieties and you can use the time while exercising as an opportunity to think about your problems in a relaxed, non-stressful way. Even a short walk can help to lift a bad mood, while regular, light to moderate exercise over a period of weeks or months has long-term positive effects on mood. What is more you can benefit from exercise whatever age you are. It has been established that people over 65 can significantly enhance their strength, stamina and flexibility within a matter of weeks of beginning a supervised exercise programme.

CHOOSING TYPES OF EXERCISE

It is important that any exercise you undertake is enjoyable and safe and that your joints are protected while exercising. There are many factors that will affect the type of exercise or activities you choose when deciding on a programme. They include your age, whether you are overweight, the nature of your illness, your existing level of fitness and factors related to your illness, such as fatigue and bone loss if you have osteoporosis. If you are under regular medical care it will be helpful to discuss a suitable exercise programme with your doctor or physiotherapist. Alternatively if

ABOVE: Although you may feel that exercising will be painful, regular exercise actually reduces pain and increases joint movement.

BELOW: A short walk is a good way to relieve stress and improve your mood.

BOTTOM: Regular light exercise will improve both your strength and stamina.

TOP: Yoga is an excellent way to strengthen and gently stretch your muscles.

ABOVE: Swimming is a low-impact aerobic exercise that is safe and effective for almost everyone. Short, regular sessions will be of most benefit.

you join a gym make sure that the instructors are aware of your condition and plan a programme that protects your joints. If you can afford it, having your own personal trainer is ideal as he or she can tailor a programme to suit you personally. Some personal trainers have a special interest in different conditions, so it is worth asking around.

There are three main types of exercise which you need to undertake for overall fitness – aerobic fitness, strength and muscular endurance, and flexibility. They are summed up in the three Ss: stamina, strength and suppleness.

People with arthritis often have weak muscles. This can be a result of the condition itself, lack of activity or it can sometimes be caused by certain drugs, such as steroids. Strong muscles help protect your bones and joints and reduce the risk of injury, and strengthening exercises can help to restore muscle and joint strength, improve your posture and strengthen your bones. Take medical advice on what exercises are advisable and do not exercise if your joints are inflamed. If it has been a while since you did any exercise you may find strengthening exercises especially hard at first but with perseverance your strength will improve. Start gently and work up gradually. Adding a few light weights can help increase muscular strength, but heavy weight-lifting is inadvisable for anyone with joint problems, and you should steer clear of weight-bearing exercises altogether, except on the advice of your doctor, if your hips and knees are painful. Yoga, which strengthens muscles gently by using your body weight when you stretch, may be preferable in this situation. Make sure that your instructor knows about your condition so that he or she can adapt asanas (postures) as necessary.

The second type of exercise, endurance or aerobic exercise, is important to increase your stamina. Aerobic means any sort of exercise that makes you feel hot and slightly breathless – things like walking, running, cycling, swimming or dancing. Aerobic exercise helps to burn off fat (important if you are overweight) and improves the strength of your heart and lungs. By improving your stamina it also helps to beat fatigue. Experts now recommend that we should all aim for 30 minutes of moderate activity most days of the week. Aerobic exercise falls into two main types – high and low impact. High-impact exercise places a greater strain on the joints and bones, so it is best for anyone with arthritis to go for low-impact aerobic activities such as swimming, aqua-aerobics, T'ai chi and walking rather than strenuous activities like aerobic classes, running, skipping or jumping. Make sure you always warm up and cool down by doing a few gentle stretches before and after an aerobic session.

The third S, suppleness, is particularly important for people with arthritis, so it's vital to do some stretching exercises. Experts often describe them as ROM – range of movement – exercises. Joints work in many different ways, as we saw in the first chapter. ROM exercises involve stretching, which lengthens and relaxes your muscles so your joints, tendons, muscles and ligaments can pass through their full range of movement – and then just a little further.

KEEPING A BALANCE

Tiredness is sometimes a problem when you first embark on an exercise programme, especially if you have been inactive for some time and have become unfit. This isn't a reason to stop exercising, but it is important to pace yourself and work up your exercise programme gradually. Try to alternate periods of rest and exercise over the course of a day and spread out periods of aerobic activity so that you balance more strenuous aerobic activities with gentler ones. Little and often is better than going on an exercise binge that tires you out and leaves you unable to do any more for a week.

Pain is difficult because, realistically speaking, you may expect to experience some stiffness or discomfort, especially if you are unused to exercising. You need to learn to listen to your body. If you feel severe or unusual pain stop what you are doing. Many people find it helpful to follow the two hour rule: if you feel more pain two hours after you have exercised than you did before you started, do less next time.

Bear in mind that, although exercise will help you to feel better straight away, it can take up to three months before you start seeing definite benefits in terms of improved stamina, strength and suppleness. This is the length of time it takes your body to adapt internally to regular exercise.

relaxation methods

Important as exercise and activity are, rest and relaxation are equally vital when you have arthritis. The key is to achieve a balance between the two. Tension makes pain worse by causing us to tighten our muscles. This in turn compresses the joints making them more stiff and painful. Relaxation on the other hand helps to slow your breathing, heart and brain waves, relaxing the muscles and reducing pain in your joints and soft tissues. You feel happier and more able to cope with the world.

Relaxation is not simply a passive process. In fact most of us are more relaxed when we are involved in some kind of activity that involves alert concentration than when we are just slumped in front of the television. Many relaxation methods involve controlling your thoughts and releasing muscular tension in order to calm the mind and the body. The secret is to have a battery of ways to relax that work for you and that you can call upon when you feel tense.

avoiding risks
check with your doctor
before embarking on an
exercise programme.

→ **Always warm up before a session. The best time to exercise is the time of day when you feel least stiff, painful and tired. This will vary from person to person.**
→ **A warm bath or shower before exercising can help relax your muscles.**
→ **Do not jerk or push your joints further than they will go when doing stretches, you should feel a gentle pull not a harsh tug.**
→ **Keep your joints soft and avoid locking them when you exercise.**
→ **Avoid the use of heavy weights. If you are advised to use weights, introduce them gradually starting with the lightest weights and always work under the supervision of a qualified instructor.**
→ **Avoid high-impact power moves such as jumping if you have rheumatoid arthritis or osteoporosis. Concentrate on gentle aerobic exercise such as walking or swimming.**
→ **Avoid exercising if your joints are actively inflamed (the signs are that they are hot, painful and swollen). You can begin exercising again once the inflammation has settled.**
→ **If any exercises cause dizziness, visual disturbances or a sudden increase in pain stop immediately.**
→ **If you have had joint surgery ask your doctor if there are any movements it would be unwise to make.**

→ Find a quiet spot where you will be undisturbed. Take the phone off the hook or put on the answerphone. Loosen any tight clothing such as ties, belts and so on and remove your shoes.

→ Sit or lie down comfortably. If you lie down you may find it helpful to place a cushion or rolled towel under your back and at your neck to relieve any distracting aches and pains.

→ Beginning at your feet gradually work your way up your body tensing and relaxing each group of muscles: toes, ankles, calves, thighs, abdomen, shoulders, back, arms, face and scalp. Tighten each muscle in turn and then feel it r-e-l-a-x. You may find it helpful to close your eyes lightly.

→ Concentrate on breathing slowly and evenly, breathing from your abdomen rather than your upper chest. To check put your hand on your abdomen and feel it rise and fall as you inhale and exhale.

→ When your body is fully relaxed, stay lying or sitting enjoying the sensation for five minutes before getting up slowly and carrying on with your daily routine.

SIMPLE RELAXATION

One very simple and widely used way of relaxing which involves contracting and relaxing the muscles is described on the left.

Once you have got used to doing this relaxation routine you can use it to help yourself relax whenever you feel tense. Get into the habit of checking yourself for signs of tension such as a furrowed brow, hunched shoulders, clenched teeth and so on and then consciously relax your muscles. You may find it helps to invest in a relaxation tape or video as an aid when you first start practising relaxation.

MEDITATION AND VISUALISATION

Meditation is an extension of relaxation. It involves stilling and concentrating the mind, which induces a feeling of relaxation and calm in the body. There are many different ways to meditate. Some involve using a mantra, a word or phrase which you repeat and concentrate on, such as the Hindu 'om', or reflecting on a quotation or an unanswerable question such as the Buddhist 'koan', 'What is the sound of one hand clapping?'. Others encourage you to focus on an object such as a flower, a candle or a picture. Many methods of meditation involve focusing on your breathing; this may be combined with counting slowly from one to five, returning to one if your attention wanders, as a way of concentrating the mind. Sometimes you are encouraged to focus on a place such as a beach, a garden, a forest or another beautiful setting, as a way of reaching a state of calm. This may be a place you have visited and where you felt relaxed or an imaginary place that you conjure up in your mind. This is known as visualization or guided imagery.

Regularly practising meditation can help you feel less anxious and more in control of your life. Research shows that during meditation the pulse and breathing slow, blood pressure falls and blood flow to the fingers and toes is increased. There is a fall in the stress hormone, cortisol, produced by the adrenal glands, and the brain's electrical activity falls into a calm, regular rhythm, known as an alpha state, akin to the moment when you fall asleep. Given that tension increases pain, which in turn increases tension, creating a vicious circle of pain and tension, it is not hard to see how the physiological changes induced by meditation can be extremely useful in helping to relax and alleviate pain in the joints or soft tissue.

SLEEP

Because sleep is so thoroughly relaxing, it can be tremendously useful in helping you feel better – both mentally and physically. Sleep allows you to rest physically and also refuels you mentally, so that you can think more positively about your condition. Different people need different amounts of sleep, so it's up to you to learn to tune into your own particular needs. Many people with arthritis and rheumatism swear by the benefits of a daytime nap, especially if their sleep has been disturbed at night. If your schedule permits it, you could try adopting the Mediterranean habit of having an afternoon siesta, but if this is not possible just a quick 10 minute nap can be sufficient to restore energy and rest the joints.

Sleep can be especially valuable if you have fibromyalgia, which is associated with sleep disturbance. Adopting a simple nightly bedtime routine, during which you wind down, will help to prime your body for sleep. For example, you could read a non-stimulating book or watch something not too demanding on television, have a relaxing bath to which you have added some soothing aromatherapy oils, and drink a cup of chamomile tea before going to bed. Keep your bedroom as a place of peace and calm where you go to rest, so you do not associate it with worries or activity.

pain control

Learning to manage your pain rather than letting it control you can be one of the most useful things you can do to help yourself feel better. We all experience pain and deal with it differently. How you personally react will depend on your personal pain threshold (the level at which you experience pain), your previous experience of pain and how you view it, as well as more immediate factors such as the weather, your surroundings, your mood and how tired and tense you are. The experience of pain can be lowered by arousal – many sports people do not feel an injury in the hurly-burly of the game, for example – or by strong emotion – in moments of extreme happiness or sadness pain may ebb away.

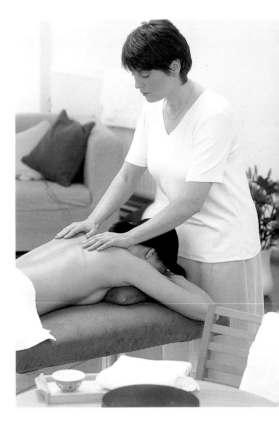

ABOVE: A professional massage can trigger the release of endorphins, the body's natural pain relief system.

the mechanism of pain

Pain exists to alert our minds to the fact that something is wrong in the body. When an injury occurs, pain messages pass along nerve pathways to the spinal cord and to the brain, which registers the sensation as pain. One of the secrets of pain control is to close the 'pain gate', blocking pain messages so that pain signals are not received by the brain. This can be achieved chemically through the use of pain-relieving drugs or naturally by stimulating the body to produce its own pain-relieving chemicals, known as endorphins.

A number of complementary therapies are thought to work by stimulating the body to produce endorphins. They include massage, aromatherapy, acupuncture and acupressure, reflexology and the use of techniques such as TENS (transcutaneous electronic nerve stimulation) – (see page 41). For more information on alternative therapies see Chapter 5.

Exercise, relaxation, a happy experience or even a warm bath can also trigger the release of endorphins. Positive thinking methods in which you acknowledge your pain but focus your thoughts outwards also help.

helping
yourself

taking control
of your pain

→ **Pay attention to your body and learn to avoid unnecessary stress on your joints.** When you lift something, always bend your knees. When you sit, pay attention to your posture, keep your abdominals gently contracted, drop your shoulders and place your feet firmly on the floor (watch the height of your chair – your shins and thighs should form a right angle when you are sitting). When talking on the phone, avoid holding the receiver between your neck and your head. If you use the phone a lot, think about getting a hands-free headset.

→ **Take regular breaks.** Avoid keeping your body in one position for any length of time, to prevent pain and stiffness. Aim to get up and move around at least every hour. If you have to stand for more than a few minutes, shift your weight from one foot to the other.

specific techniques for pain control

HEAT TREATMENT

The application of heat is a tried and tested way of relaxing muscles and reducing pain. Heat treatments can include taking a warm bath or shower, whirlpools, the use of a heat lamp, heating pad or paraffin wax treatments, Turkish baths (steam rooms) or saunas. Check with the doctor before using a steam room or sauna as it may be contraindicated if you have other medical conditions such as high blood pressure or heart disease. Simple measures such as warming your bed with an electric blanket before getting into it or before getting up (if you suffer from morning stiffness), using flannelette sheets or warming your clothes on the radiator or in the airing cupboard can all also help.

COLD TREATMENT (cryotherapy)

Cold is especially helpful in quelling inflammation, reducing swelling and relieving pain. The various methods of applying cold to the body include cold baths and showers, cold gel-packs and simply wrapping a bag of ice cubes or frozen peas in a towel. Place the cold object against the affected area for 10–15 minutes but do not keep it on too long to avoid cold 'burns'. Wrapping the cold object in a towel or thin piece of cloth should prevent this.

SPLINTING

Supporting a damaged joint with a splint can help in some instances if the pain is very severe. Ask your doctor or physiotherapist about choosing one that is suitable for you.

→ **Know yourself**. Overdoing things can lead to fatigue and flare-ups. However underactivity can lead to boredom, depression and muscle weakness. Learn to listen to your body and plan your day so that you get the amount of activity and rest that suits you. Prioritize what you have to do by keeping lists, so that you cut unnecessary tasks to the minimum. You will be more efficient if you break up your day rather than going full pelt all the time. Tune into your body rhythms and plan your day accordingly. Many people feel most alert in the morning, so should plan to do tasks that require most concentration then. Remember you also need some time off simply to enjoy yourself.

→ **Don't be afraid to seek help**. No one is going to award you any medals for suffering in silence. If you need help, then ask for it. Most people are only too happy to be of assistance and you can reciprocate the favour when you are feeling well enough.

ABOVE: By planning your day around the times you are most alert, you will be able to participate more fully in any activity.

TENS (transcutaneous electrical nerve stimulation)

TENS works by sending electrical impulses to the brain which block pain messages and stimulates the release of the body's own pain-relieving chemicals, endorphins. TENS machines consist of a small hand-held box with four electrodes, which can be placed on particular points to block the sensation of pain. You may feel a sensation of vibration or pins and needles, which changes to a continuous electrical sensation. Alternatively you may feel nothing at all. TENS has been found to be especially useful for back or neck pain or localized joint pain. Consult your doctor before using TENS. It should not be used if you have a pacemaker or are in the early months of pregnancy.

SELF-MASSAGE

Massage helps to warm and relax the body, stimulating increased blood supply to the tissues and inducing deep feelings of calm that help trigger the production of pain-relieving endorphins. Self-massage can do much to help frozen shoulders, neck stiffness and shoulder tension, while massaging around a painful, inflamed joint (never massage directly over the joint) can help to improve circulation and provide pain relief. There are various massage techniques that can be used, including stroking, kneading, pummelling and knuckling. However any stroke that feels good will do. For quick relief, you can massage over your clothes. Alternatively you might like to massage the skin directly using oil to help your hands glide over the skin. Essential oils of chamomile and lavender help relieve inflammation. Use two or three drops in a teaspoon of a carrier oil such as almond oil. Do not continue massaging if pain develops. For tips on how to massage, invest in a good book on massage or enroll on a massage course.

This chapter covers **all the methods your doctor and other medical professionals may use** to help control your condition. Many people with arthritis and rheumatism have their condition controlled by drugs, both first-line and second-line drugs. First-line drugs are those that **treat the symptoms of the disease, such as painkillers and anti-inflammatories**. Second-line drugs help to slow the disease, **helping to keep you fitter for longer and reducing the risk of permanent damage** to joints, tendons and muscles.

Other orthodox medical treatments include physiotherapy, **designed to help the joints stay as mobile as possible** and reduce pain. In extreme cases, surgery may be used to treat your condition. All these methods of treatment have a place and your medical practitioner will try to devise the best regimen for you.

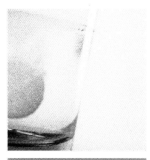

the orthodox
approach

drug treatment

Numerous drugs are used to treat arthritis and rheumatism and different drugs are used to treat different conditions. Broadly speaking, drugs fall into two types. The first type – known as first-line drugs – are those which control symptoms and are used for most types of arthritis. These include pain-killers (analgesics) and non-steroidal anti-inflammatory drugs (NSAIDs). The second type of drugs – known as second-line drugs or disease-modifying antirheumatic drugs (DMARDs) – are those which can actually slow the disease process. When prescribed early on, they can make a real difference in helping you stay healthier for longer and prevent permanent joint and tissue damage. Because they are slow acting, DMARDs are usually prescribed in combination with an NSAID or corticosteroid drug. These drugs are specific to the particular type of arthritis or rheumatism and will be tailored to you and your condition. So, for example, if you have rheumatoid arthritis you will be prescribed different drugs to someone who has, say, gout. You may also be prescribed different drugs to someone else with rheumatoid arthritis. Taking more than one DMARD at a time can enhance their benefits and in recent years doctors have increasingly been prescribing DMARDs in combinations of two and even three.

Most drugs used for the treatment of arthritis and rheumatism are oral preparations that you take by mouth. However some such as gold are given by injection. Others may be given in the form of a suppository. It is common to be prescribed a 'cocktail' of different drugs. For example if you have rheumatoid arthritis a typical combination might be a painkiller, a non-steroidal anti-inflammatory drug and a disease-modifying drug such as methotrexate.

It is worth bearing in mind that drugs can sometimes take several weeks or even months before producing an improvement in symptoms. Try to be patient if you do not appear to be experiencing immediate relief. If you find you are not being helped by a drug your doctor has prescribed do not just stop taking it. Tell your doctor. It could be that the drug you have been prescribed is a slow-acting one and needs time to work. There may be a degree of trial and error before the precise combination of drugs and treatments that best controls your condition is found. This can be frustrating and demoralising, especially if a drug that has previously seemed to be effective stops controlling your condition as well as before. Do not despair. Treatments are changing all the time and with patience and perseverance it will be possible to find the most effective treatment for you.

Most drugs used to treat arthritis and rheumatism fall into a few well-defined categories, which work in similar ways, although there may be subtle differences in the way they act. How well a particular drug works and the way if affects you will depend on several factors, such as your

BELOW: Several different drugs are often prescribed together to treat arthritic conditions. Ask your doctor what each of them is for and how long it should be before you notice an improvement in your symptoms.

age, your sex, your weight and also any other health problems you may have. Your doctor will take all these factors into account when assessing the medication regimen which is best suited to you.

side effects and limitations

There is no such thing as the perfect drug. By definition a drug is a substance that changes the body's chemistry. For this reason all drugs (including over-the-counter medications and 'natural' remedies such as herbs) involve risks as well as benefits and those used to treat arthritis and rheumatism are no exception. It is helpful to know what side effects to expect so that if you develop unexpected ones you can report them to your doctor.

When prescribing a particular drug the doctor will try to weigh the benefits for your arthritis or rheumatism against the disadvantages of any potentially harmful effects. Sometimes he or she may consider that the risks of a drug outweigh the benefits you are likely to experience. If you have a stomach ulcer, for example, the doctor is likely to decide against prescribing a non-steroidal anti-inflammatory drug such as ibuprofen, which can irritate the ulcer. However in other cases the doctor may feel that the risks of the side effects are outweighed by the potential benefits of the drug. This may be the case with some of the immunosuppressant drugs listed below. Before prescribing a particular treatment your doctor will explain what side effects you are likely to expect.

Although it can be alarming to read about side effects, bear in mind, first, that not all side effects affect everyone who is prescribed a particular drug and, second, that many subside once your body has got used to the drug. Some side effects such as stomach upsets and rashes are more of a nuisance than a serious problem and some can be minimized by simple self-help measures. For example, taking NSAIDs with a meal can help buffer their stomach-irritating effects and taking folic acid if you are prescribed methotrexate can reduce the risk of developing mouth ulcers, stomach irritation and diarrhoea.

However some side effects are potentially more serious. Some of the second-line drugs used to treat arthritis can affect levels of blood cells and kidney function. Where this is the case your doctor will arrange for regular safety checks, such as blood and liver function tests to be carried out, so that if a drug is causing potentially harmful side effects it can be discontinued before it has done any serious damage.

If you have been prescribed a particular drug which doesn't agree with you don't just grin and bear it, go back to the doctor and ask whether the side effects are likely to subside or if he or she can prescribe a different preparation.

medication checklist

→ Always make sure you understand what each drug you have been prescribed is for and what side effects you can expect.

→ Make sure you know how many times a day you should take the drug and how it should be taken.

→ If you are taking several different types of tablets you may find it convenient to get a special dispenser which you load with your daily drugs.

→ Never share your medication with other people or take their medication.

→ Keep all medication out of the reach of children.

→ Always take medication exactly as prescribed. For example anti-inflammatory drugs should always be taken with or after food, while penicillamine, a drug used to treat rheumatoid arthritis, is taken on an empty stomach.

→ Check the pack for any special instructions, for example some drugs should not be taken with alcohol.

→ Make sure you don't keep any tablets beyond their use-by date.

→ If you are in any doubt about any aspect of your medication, check with the doctor or pharmacist.

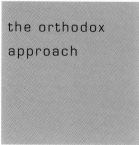

the orthodox
approach

drugs you may be prescribed

Below is a run-down of the main groups of drugs that may be used to treat arthritis and rheumatic conditions, looking at how they work and what side effects you may experience. It is intended as a general rather than a definitive guide. For further information consult your medical practitioner.

first-line drugs

First-line drugs are used in almost all forms of arthritic disease. They are the drugs that treat the symptoms of these conditions, such as pain, inflammation of the joints and membranes, and swelling. First-line drugs are the painkillers, NSAIDs and corticosteroids.

PAINKILLERS (analgesics)

common drugs
Paracetamol, co-codamol, co-proxamol, co-dydramol

Analgesic drugs are used to quell pain. They can range from simple drugs that most people have in their medicine cabinets, such as paracetamol, to combinations of paracetamol with a stronger painkiller such as codeine, and other preparations. They are often used to enhance the pain-alleviating effects of other medicines.

SIDE EFFECTS

Paracetamol is a tried and tested painkiller and side effects are not usually troublesome, although it is important not to exceed the stated dose as this can cause liver damage. Some of the stronger compound painkillers may cause side effects such drowsiness, constipation, dizziness, nausea, rashes or, rarely, breathing difficulties.
It is important to be aware of what is in the tablets you are taking so that you do not accidentally overdose by taking other medicines containing the same ingredients (for example, over-the-counter cold remedies containing paracetamol). Always tell the pharmacist what medications you have been prescribed when buying any over-the-counter remedies.

PAINKILLING CREAMS AND LOTIONS

A whole range of creams, lotions, gels and sprays which you apply to the skin are available over the counter to help ease pain. Some contain substances such as menthol, which act by producing counter irritation which distracts you from the pain, others contain salicylates (the chemical found in aspirin) and are absorbed through the skin to reduce inflammation. Capsaicin is a cream or lotion made from chilli pepper seeds that works by depleting a chemical called Substance P in the nerve endings, preventing pain signals from being sent to the brain. It can also reduce inflammation in RA. Used three or four times a day, it is said to be extremely effective, however it can take a month before an improvement is felt. Always wash your hands well after using a painkilling cream and never use one on broken or irritated skin. If you have an allergic reaction to aspirin check with the doctor before using salicylate-based painkilling creams.

reducing the side effects of NSAIDs

→ Always take your tablets with or after meals to buffer their effects.

→ Drink a glass of water with your tablets.

→ Avoid alcohol as much as possible.

→ Stop smoking.

→ If you do experience side effects stop taking the drug and get in touch with your doctor as soon as possible.

RIGHT: When taking oral medicines, check with your pharmacist exactly when to take them: most should be taken with food, but a few are better taken on an empty stomach.

NON-STEROIDAL ANTI-INFLAMMATORY DRUGS (NSAIDs)

common drugs

Ibuprofen, naproxen, indomethacin, piroxicam, diclofenac, meloxicam, nabumetone

NSAIDs are painkillers that also act to reduce inflammation and swelling. This in turn helps to relieve pain and stiffness and so improves mobility. Where inflammation is not present, for example in osteoarthritis, a simple painkiller will usually suffice.

NSAIDs are prescribed for many different types of arthritis often in combination with other drugs or painkillers. Some types are taken several times a day others are slow release preparations which, as the name suggests, release their ingredients slowly into the blood stream over a period of time. The doctor will usually prescribe a low dose at first and increase the dose as necessary. There are many different NSAIDs and if one doesn't work for you another one usually will. NSAIDs are usually taken orally as a tablet or capsule but some come as a liquid, a fizzy tablet or a suppository.

SIDE EFFECTS

Many people tolerate NSAIDs well, however they can sometimes cause mild headaches, drowsiness and dizziness when you first start taking them. These usually wear off as your body gets used to the drug.

Larger doses can have more troublesome effects including nausea, indigestion, gastrointestinal bleeding, diarrhoea, rashes and wheezing. Caution is needed if you have a peptic ulcer, or if you have history of asthma because NSAIDs can trigger attacks of wheezing, so make sure your doctor is aware of this. Some people who are allergic to aspirin may also experience an adverse reaction to NSAIDs, so you should tell your doctor if this applies to you.

Because NSAIDs can aggravate or even trigger the development of a peptic ulcer the doctor may prescribe an anti-ulcer drug such as Zantac to be taken in combination with a NSAID. Some arthritis drugs, such as Arthrotec, contain a combination of a NSAID, in this case diclofenac sodium, and an anti-ulcer drug, misoprostol, in one tablet, to protect the stomach lining. Side effects may include stomach upsets, heavy periods, headaches, dizziness, nausea, swelling and skin reactions.

RIGHT: NSAIDs occasionally cause side effects such as headaches when you first start taking them, but persevere as they should soon disappear.

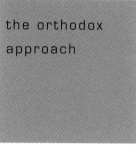

the orthodox
approach

RIGHT: Corticosteroids can occasionally have severe side effects when taken in large quantities, so your doctor will keep a close watch on your health, including your blood pressure.

CORTICOSTEROID DRUGS (steroids)

common drugs
Prednisone, cortisone, methylprednisone, triamcinolone

Corticosteroids – often referred to simply as steroids – are a group of drugs which are similar in their chemical structure to the natural hormone, cortisone, produced by the adrenal cortex in the brain. They work by reducing the production of hormone-like substances called prostaglandins that are involved in the process of inflammation and have an anti-inflammatory effect. They also suppress the immune system by reducing the release and activity of the white blood cells. This makes them especially useful for treating arthritic and rheumatic conditions in which there is inflammation, such as rheumatoid arthritis, polymyalgia rheumatica and lupus.

SIDE EFFECTS

The main problem with oral steroids is that when used in high doses over long periods they can produce serious side effects such as thinning of the bones, oedema (accumulation of fluid in the tissues), weight gain, mood changes, diabetes, high blood pressure, cataracts and an increased susceptibility to infection because they suppress the body's immune system. For this reason the doctor will only use steroids when strictly necessary and in as low a dose as possible.

HOW STERIODS ARE USED

Where only one or a few joints are affected corticosteroids are highly effective given by injection into the joint (intra-articular injection) to relieve local pain, swelling and inflammation. The advantage is that side effects are kept to a minimum because the drug is concentrated in one place, although some people may experience a loss of fatty tissue or skin colour at the site of the injection.

Steroids can also be given by injection into a muscle or vein (intramuscular or intravenous injection) to quell a severe flare-up of inflammation. They may also be prescribed as a daily tablet to quell more general inflammation in cases of rheumatoid arthritis, lupus and polymyalgia rheumatica. The most common steroid of this kind is a highly effective drug called prednisolone, which will usually improve symptoms within a matter of days. It is usually taken once a day, with or after breakfast, although it can also be useful for people experiencing morning stiffness when taken at night.

The doctor will try to prescribe the lowest dose possible to improve your symptoms. However higher doses may be needed to treat rare complications of rheumatoid arthritis such as arteritis (inflammation of the arteries).

Because corticosteroids suppress production of the body's own corticosteroid hormones you must never stop taking them abruptly. Always lower the dose gradually and carry a steroid card or wear a Medic Alert bracelet.

second-line disease-modifying anti-rheumatic drugs (DMARDS)

common drugs

Anti-malarial drugs, penicillamine, gold, immunosuppressant drugs such as methotrexate, cyclosporin and azathioprine.

DMARDs work in different ways to slow or suppress the disease process within the joints. Although they are often highly effective, they tend to work slowly and it will often be weeks or months before any improvement is noticed. Because most of these drugs are extremely powerful they may also cause potentially more harmful side effects, so if you are prescribed them the doctor will want to monitor you carefully to ensure that serious side effects do not occur.

ABOVE: Most second-line drugs have possible, if rare, side effects, so contact your doctor if any other symptoms appear while you are taking them.

ANTI-MALARIAL DRUGS

common drugs

Hydroxychloroquine, chloroquine

It may seem strange but anti-malarial drugs are some of the most useful medications for reducing disease activity and inflammation in rheumatoid arthritis. They are also useful for treating lupus, which can be triggered by sunlight, due to their UV light-blocking properties.

Like many of the second-line drugs used to treat arthritis, anti-malarials can take up to three or six months to produce a significant improvement, although some benefits may be seen within 4–6 weeks. They are taken once or twice a day with food to avoid nausea.

SIDE EFFECTS

Of all the drugs used to treat arthritis anti-malarial drugs are among the safest and least likely to cause side effects. Scientists still don't understand exactly how this group of drugs quells the disease process in arthritis but they are highly effective.
Although anti-malarial drugs are some of the safest used to treat RA, potential side effects may include indigestion, diarrhoea, headaches, skin rashes and blurred vision.
In the past high doses were used which could cause serious damage to the eyesight but such problems are unlikely with today's low doses.

PENICILLAMINE

An anti-rheumatic drug used to reduce inflammation and so ease swelling and stiffness in rheumatoid arthritis. The drug can take up to six months before it is effective. Because it can react with food you will usually be told to take it an hour before or after eating.

SIDE EFFECTS

Penicillamine can cause allergic rashes, itching, nausea, diarrhoea, a temporary loss of taste, a metallic taste when eating or unusual-smelling urine. More seriously, although rarely, it can reduce the number of white blood cells and platelets in the blood or cause impaired kidney function. For this reason the doctor will perform regular blood and urine tests when you are taking the drug.

RIGHT: Immunosuppressant drugs such as azathioprine can cause side effects like jaundice, rashes and bruising, so your doctor will keep a close check on your skin.

GOLD

Gold is the common name for sodium aurothiomalate. It is an extremely powerful treatment that works by reducing inflammation, which makes it useful for rheumatoid arthritis, psoriatic arthritis and palindromic arthritis, especially if NSAIDs have proved ineffective in relieving symptoms. However it can have serious side effects so the doctor will want to monitor you carefully while you are taking it.

Gold may be given by intramuscular injection into your buttock or as a tablet. Injections are usually given weekly at first and it may take from three to six months before an improvement is seen. If it does prove effective injections may be given at less frequent intervals after this. In tablet form gold is taken daily with food. Like intramuscular gold, it can take from three to six months before any improvement is noticed.

SIDE EFFECTS

Gold given by injection can cause dermatitis and alopecia (hair loss). More seriously it can cause bone marrow damage, which can result in low levels of white blood cells or platelets, and kidney damage, so blood and urine tests will be performed before each injection. Occasionally gold injections can cause a severe life-threatening reaction called anaphylactic shock. For this reason the doctor will give a trial dose before prescribing a course of gold. You are recommended to remain in the surgery or clinic for a short time after each injection has been given so emergency treatment can be given if necessary.

IMMUNOSUPPRESSANT DRUGS

common drugs
Azathioprine, cyclophosphamide, cyclosporine, methotrexate

Immunosuppressant drugs act to quell the activity of the body's own defence mechanism, the immune system. This ability makes them especially useful in both rheumatoid arthritis and lupus, in which the immune system is overactive.

Many immunosuppressant drugs were originally used to help prevent the body rejecting transplanted organs. Some of these drugs are also cytotoxic (cell-killing) drugs, originally used to kill cancerous cells.

Although they are effective, great care needs to be taken if you are prescribed immunosuppressant drugs as they can be highly toxic and cause several unpleasant side effects (see chart opposite). The doctor will usually start you on a low dose, calculated by your body weight, and may adjust the dose, depending on how you react to the drug. You are likely to need regular blood and, possibly, liver function tests to monitor toxicity and side effects.

immunosuppressant drugs

DRUG	USED FOR	SIDE EFFECT AND CAUTIONS
Azathioprine	Lupus, rheumatoid arthritis, polymyalgia rheumatica (with steroids to reduce dose of steroids)	Nausea, loss of appetite. More rarely weakness, fatigue, jaundice, rash or fever, bruising or bleeding. The doctor will order regular blood tests as the drug can lower the number of white blood cells and platelets, causing increased vulnerability to infections, bruising and bleeding. Tests for liver function should also be performed.
Cyclo-phosphamide	Rheumatoid arthritis, lupus, vasculitis	Nausea, inflammation and bleeding of the bladder (haemorrhagic cystitis). More rarely hair loss, irregular periods and mouth ulcers. Risk of anaemia because the drug reduces the number of red blood cells. Risk of herpes zoster (shingles) due to lowered immunity. Sterility in men, and fertility can be affected in women. It can also trigger premature menopause and increased risk of osteoporosis. Regular blood tests should be done to check for toxicity. You should avoid contact with infections.
Cyclosporin	Rheumatoid arthritis	Raised blood pressure, nausea, fatigue, diarrhoea, swollen gums, increased hair growth, reduced kidney function, tremor, burning hands and feet (this usually disappears). Regular blood tests and blood pressure checks are needed.
Methotrexate	Rheumatoid arthritis, psoriatic arthritis	Skin rashes, itching, sore mouth, mouth ulcers, nausea, vomiting, diarrhoea. Regular blood tests should be performed to check for bone marrow or liver damage. You should avoid alcohol or limit consumption as methotrexate can affect the liver. If you develop a temperature, unexplained bruising, cough or shortness of breath contact the doctor immediately as methotrexate can cause lung disease.

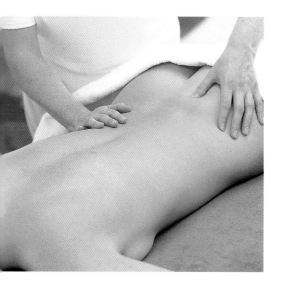

ABOVE: Physiotherapy improves mobility.

antidepressants

As we have seen, anxiety can intensify pain and this in turn can trigger depression. Antidepressants can help break this vicious cycle. Taken at night before going to bed they can help you get a better night's sleep. Antidepressant drugs of the tricyclic group such as amitriptyline and nortriptyline are often especially useful in alleviating the pain of fibromyalgia. The doctor will usually avoid prescribing conventional sleeping pills, as they can be habit forming and often do not produce a better quality of sleep. It can take up to eight weeks for tricyclics to become fully effective, so it is worth persevering even if they are not effective at first.

SIDE EFFECTS

The most common side effects include a dry mouth, blurred vision, dizziness, daytime drowsiness, constipation and difficulty passing urine. However these usually wane as treatment continues. In order to minimize side effects the doctor will usually start you on a low dose and raise it to the most appropriate level.

physiotherapy

Physiotherapy can be useful in helping your joints to be as pain-free and mobile as possible. The physiotherapist can help develop an exercise programme tailored to your needs and may also use techniques such as massage, ultrasound, TENS (transcutaneous electrical nerve stimulation), hydrotherapy (water treatment) and various hot and cold therapies to control pain.

types of surgery

SYNOVECTOMY	**ARTHRODESIS** (fusing the bones to stabilize a joint)
In this operation the lining of the joint, the synovium, which becomes inflamed in inflammatory types of arthritis such as RA, is removed surgically. The operation can reduce pain and swelling and may delay the destruction of cartilage and bone. However it is not a cure; inflammation and pain may return after surgery as the joint-lining tissue starts to regrow.	In this operation the joint is fixed permanently to improve stability and reduce pain. The surgeon removes a thin layer of tissue from the ends of the two bones and fixes them together either by grafting or by using a pin, rod or plate. As new bone cells grow the two bones fuse together. The joint cannot move and therefore arthrodesis is usually used when joint replacement is not appropriate or possible. It is most often used in the spine, wrist, ankle and foot.

non-drug treatment

Surgery can bring relief from arthritis, when other treatments have failed. Surgical techniques are most beneficial for people with severe rheumatoid and osteoarthritis and less frequently for people with ankylosing spondilitis and psoriatic arthritis. If you have less severe rheumatoid or osteoarthritis, gout or one of the rheumatic conditions you are unlikely to need surgery.

new treatment approaches

A wide range of new drug treatments, surgical and non-surgical interventions are currently being investigated. Potential new drug treatments include viscosupplements, given by injection, which contain a synthetic form of a natural joint lubricant and shock absorber; biologic response modifiers, injectable drugs which block the action of a substance involved in triggering inflammation and tissue damage; new disease-modifying drugs with fewer side effects than those currently in use; and cox-2 inhibitors, drugs which are similar to NSAIDs but which are kinder to the stomach.

Surgeons are also developing new operations. These include the use of microsurgery, cartilage transplants and a new procedure called periosteal transplantation in which cells used to produce cartilage are inserted into the joint to regenerate the cartilage and heal the surface. Although many of these treatments are not yet ready, they offer real hope for the future.

New non-surgical techniques are also being developed to ease pain and restore bone. They include alternatives to corticosteroid injections and a technique which removes antibodies that cause inflammation.

drug treatment for gout

Acute attacks are treated by NSAIDs. Occasionally, if these don't help, the doctor may prescribe other drugs including corticosteroids. However if you are prone to gout the doctor may give you a preventive drug to control levels of uric acid (which is produced in excess in gout). The most common is allopurinol, a drug with an excellent safety record. Its only common side effect is a rash, which vanishes after treatment. Other preventive drugs include probenecid and sulphinpyrazone which work by flushing uric acid through the kidneys.

OSTEOTOMY

In this operation the surgeon cuts the bone next to a painful or damaged joint and repositions it to correct deformity and relieve pain. Because body weight is distributed more evenly across the joint the operation can help reduce cartilage damage and stimulate healing. It is used mainly in the knee and foot in osteoarthritis.

ARTHROPLASTY (joint replacement)

If a joint is severely damaged by osteo- or rheumatoid arthritis, replacement with an artificial joint can give a new lease of life. The surgeon removes all or part of the damaged joint and replaces it with a plastic or metal joint, or prosthesis, to use the medical term.

The hip is the most common joint replacement but prostheses can also be used to replace shoulder, finger, elbow, ankle, knee and other joints.

Although artificial joints have a limited lifespan, materials are getting better all the time and arthroplasty can bring dramatic relief from pain and return joints almost to normal when all else has failed.

Complementary treatments can do an enormous amount to help you think more positively and help alleviate some of the symptoms of your arthritis or rheumatism. Many people with these conditions seek complementary or alternative therapies because they are disappointed that mainstream medicine has not cured their condition and hope that complementary medicine will be the answer. This is not a good reason for seeking complementary help. You have to accept that many types of arthritis and rheumatism are long-term conditions which you have to learn to live with.

Although complementary therapies can help with factors such as pain control, relaxation and relieving fatigue, they cannot perform miracles and you should be wary of any practitioner who claims that they can. However, **used alongside orthodox treatment, a number of complementary therapies can be of real help as well as offering you the opportunity to play a more active part in controlling your condition**. Their emphasis on treating the whole person provides a more individual, personal approach, which takes into account factors such as your personality, lifestyle and your emotional and spiritual needs and how these affect your symptoms.

complementary
treatments

choosing a therapy

There is a huge number of complementary treatments on offer and it can be difficult to choose the one most appropriate for you, especially as not as much research has been done on them as it has on conventional therapies. As a rule, choosing a therapy or therapies that you personally find appealing is likely to enhance your sense of control and of doing something positive for yourself.

This chapter outlines what is involved in some of the therapies that have been found to be helpful in arthritis and rheumatism, to help you make a choice. If you would like to try a therapy that is not included try to find out as much as you can about it before you sign up for treatment. On the whole it is best to go for the gentler complementary therapies and to avoid anything that is harsh or invasive. For example, massage is often helpful but it is better to go for an aromatherapy massage rather than a more vigorous type like rolfing.

ALEXANDER TECHNIQUE

Being in constant pain makes you tense, which affects your posture and the way you use your body. This in turn creates further stress on the joints. The Alexander Technique can be extremely effective in dealing with osteoarthritis and rheumatoid arthritis and is also useful in relieving fatigue and lethargy, anxiety, back, neck and joint pain. It involves learning to use your body in a more efficient and natural way. Contracted muscles are released, joints are freed and the spine is lengthened. Improved use of the body reduces mechanical interference and strain, and enhances the body's own healing powers. The Technique is taught in a series of one-to-one lessons during which the teacher looks at the way you hold yourself while doing everyday movements such as sitting, standing, walking, bending, talking and lifting. The teacher will then guide and direct you into ways of using your body better.

LEFT: Rather than treating specific symptoms, the Alexander Technique aims to retrain the body into moving in a natural manner. This is often found to relieve stress around the joints.

AROMATHERAPY

Aromatherapy can be particularly helpful for stress and anxiety and muscular and rheumatic aches and pains. It involves the use of essential oils, aromatic essences extracted from plants, flowers, trees, fruit, bark, grasses and seeds, which have distinct therapeutic, psychological and physiological effects. There are about 150 essential oils each with its own scent and healing property. Some are anti-inflammatory, some are pain relieving, some are stimulating, some relaxing. Others have effects on the mind such as lifting depression. The oils can be inhaled either directly, in steam or in a special diffuser or vaporizer. They are often used in massage, which combines the benefits of the oil with touch, to relax, improve circulation and release energy from tense muscles. Oils can also be used in baths and compresses.

The essential oil molecules are absorbed through the skin from where they travel in the blood stream around the body. The oils work on the limbic system, a part of the brain that is associated with mood, emotion and memory. In this way they can have a positive, encouraging effect and help lift depression. Useful oils for arthritis and rheumatism include geranium oil for its uplifting effects, ginger oil to warm, juniper to help remove toxins, and rosemary to encourage circulation and remove toxins.

Caution is also needed with herbal treatments if you are taking conventional drugs. Herbs can have powerful pharmacological effects, just like conventional drugs, and may have potential harmful reactions with conventional medication. For this reason it is always best to seek the help of a qualified herbal practitioner rather than treating yourself. You should also inform your doctor if you are taking any herbal remedies.

choosing a therapist

Because anyone can set themselves up as a complementary practitioner the onus is on you to make sure you choose someone who is trained and qualified. A growing number of practitioners are now registered with a professional body, so check their credentials. In the UK you can do this through the Institute of Complementary Medicine, which keeps a list of accredited practitioners. Beware of anyone who offers you a miracle cure.

using essential oils

Massage: Dilute five drops of essential oil in a carrier oil such as sweet almond or grapeseed oil.
Baths: Add up to eight drops to a bath.
Compresses: Place one to two drops in a bowl of warm water. Soak a piece of cotton in the water and wring it out then place it over the affected area. Cover with a warm towel and leave for two hours.

REFLEXOLOGY

Reflexology, or zone therapy, involves applying pressure to various points on the feet, and sometimes the hands, to stimulate the body's own healing mechanisms and improve physical and mental health. Reflexologists believe that various points on the foot correspond to different parts of the body and the organs. By applying pressure to these areas, blockages can be released and energy is rebalanced in the corresponding body part or organ. It is a safe and relaxing treatment that can be helpful for relieving pain, lifting stress and fatigue and increasing well-being.

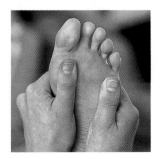

BELOW: Reflexology is a very safe, pain-relieving treatment. You will need just a few sessions for mild pain, more for acute problems. Your feet may feel a little sore after a session.

AYURVEDIC MEDICINE

Ayurveda is a Sanskrit word meaning the science of life. It is a complete and complex system of medicine developed in India over 3,000 years ago. Treatments can include detoxification, fasting, diet, exercise, herbs, yoga, meditation, massage with herbal oils and other methods designed to enhance your mental and emotional health. Intriguingly, fasting has been shown to improve the symptoms of RA when used in western medicine.

In Ayurvedic medicine each person has a unique constitution determined by the balance of three vital energies known as doshas, which are known by their Sanskrit names of vátha, pitha and kapha. In Ayurvedic medicine good health depends on eating a healthy diet, exercise, healthy elimination and balanced emotional and physical health. Ill health is said to be caused by imbalance of the doshas and good health is restored by means of detoxification followed by the use of herbal or mineral remedies to correct the imbalance. Spices and herbs that may be prescribed for arthritis include cumin, coriander, turmeric and boswellia serrata, which comes from an Indian tree. In animal studies boswellia inhibits inflammation and prevents loss of a protein found in cartilage. During clinical trials carried out in India, a significant proportion of people treated with boswellia showed improvement in rheumatoid arthritis symptoms.

herbs to help arthritis

ABOVE: Devil's claw is used to treat digestive problems as well as rheumatism and arthritis. It should not be taken during pregnancy.

Devil's claw (harpagophytum procumbens, a South African plant), is said to help relieve pain and inflammation in arthritis and several scientific studies have been done, although none has been conclusive. The herb contains glycosides, powerful anti-inflammatory agents.

Ginger is said to have anti-inflammatory effects similar to NSAIDs. Other anti-inflammatory herbs include aloe vera, bogbean, feverfew, primula and willow. Wild yam and lignum vitae are said to help relieve attacks of rheumatoid arthritis.

Because arthritis and rheumatism are complex conditions you should not treat yourself with herbal remedies but see a qualified herbalist who has the training to know which herbs are most appropriate. Never take herbal treatments when you are pregnant unless they are prescribed by a medical herbalist and make sure your doctor and your herbalist are fully informed about all the medications you are taking.

CHINESE MEDICINE

Chinese medicine is a complete system of traditional medicine. It includes the use of acupuncture and acupressure, exercise techniques such as Qi gong and T'ai chi, and the use of Chinese herbs.

According to the theory, good health depends on a balance of two vital qualities known as yin and yang. Yin is the dark, passive, feminine, cold, negative principle, while yang is the light, active, masculine, warm, positive principle. Inner harmony depends on keeping a free flow of the body's life force, known as qi or chi, which flows along meridians through the body. Each meridian is linked to an organ or function such as the lungs, kidneys or gallbladder. When chi flows freely through the meridians the body is balanced and healthy. If chi becomes sluggish or blocked this can produce mental, physical or emotional ill health. Various things, including the weather, what you eat and how you live, can affect the balance of chi.

ACUPUNCTURE AND ACUPRESSURE

Acupuncture and acupressure (finger pressure) are designed to restore the healthy flow of chi by stimulating points along the meridians. Acupuncture has strong painkilling effects, which makes it useful for treating the pain of arthritis. It can also reduce inflammation and improve mobility. In Western medical terms it is thought that acupuncture's pain relieving effects may work by closing the pain 'gate' and sparking the release of endorphins, the body's own painkilling chemicals. Acupuncture is said to be especially effective when started in the early stages of arthritis.

CHINESE HERBS

Chinese herbs used to treat arthritis include tripterygium wilfordii, or thunder god vine. In tests carried out in the US this plant has been found to quell inflammation or the body's immune response. Certain parts of the plant are toxic, so caution is advised. If you consult a Chinese practitioner make sure you get regular blood and urine tests to check for lowered blood count or kidney damage.

T'AI CHI CHUAN

Usually known simply as T'ai chi, which translates as 'the supreme way of the fist', T'ai chi chuan is a non-combatic martial art that includes meditation and exercise to promote health. Regular practice de-stresses the muscles and nervous system and improves posture and joint flexibility. T'ai chi takes the form of a set of slow-moving, graceful exercises, performed in a pattern to encourage relaxation and harmony of the mind and body by rebalancing the flow of chi. T'ai chi has been shown to help with anxiety, depression, muscle strength and mobility.

homoeopathic remedies

ABOVE: Some herbalists will prepare the herbs for you, others will simply give you a prescription that you can take to a herb-dispensing shop.

Homoeopathic remedies come in the form of tiny milk sugar tablets, pills, granules, powders or tinctures. Homoeopaths believe it is the energy or 'vibrational pattern' of the remedy rather than its chemical content that stimulates healing, by activating the body's own vital energy. Thus remedies are diluted to the extent that even toxic substances have no harmful effect. Extracts are dissolved in a mixture of alcohol and water and left to stand for 2–4 weeks before being strained. The solution, or mother tincture, is then diluted sometimes many thousands of times to make different potencies. Intriguingly in homoeopathic medicine, the lower the amount of active ingredient the higher potency and the greater its healing power. Between dilutions the remedies are shaken. It is this which is said to transfer the energy of the remedy to the mixture.

HERBAL TREATMENT (Western herbalism)

Extracts of plants and herbs have been used to heal in every culture since the beginning of time. In fact herbs and their derivatives are the basis of many modern medicines including some of those used to treat arthritis and rheumatism. Unlike conventional medicine where the active ingredient is extracted from the plant, in herbal medicine the whole plant is used. This is said to be safer in that herbs and plants often contain buffering ingredients, which help prevent side effects, as well as the pharmacologically active ingredient.

Herbs are classified in a similar way to drugs. Thus some are anti-inflammatory, some painkilling and so on. There are also a group of herbs known as adaptogens which help to restore the natural balance of the body. Unlike medical drugs, herbs are often prescribed to support the body while it heals itself, rather than to relieve symptoms. Remedies come in the form of tinctures, creams, compresses, poultices, infusions (teas made using the flowers, leaves or green stems of plants), decoctions of roots, barks, nuts and seeds, oils to be used in herbal baths, and as tablets or capsules.

Chronic conditions such as arthritis are likely to need several appointments with a herbalist, especially if you have had the condition for a while. A herbalist cannot reverse the damage done by the disease but he or she can alleviate symptoms and improve well-being.

HOMOEOPATHY

Homoeopathy works on the principle that 'like cures like'. This means that substances that cause the symptoms of illness in a well person are given to cure similar symptoms in someone who is ill. There are over 2,000 homoeopathic remedies made with natural ingredients from animal, vegetable and mineral sources.

Homoeopaths treat the whole person and like other complementary practitioners they will also advise on diet and lifestyle to support the body as it heals itself. For example a homoeopath may advise you to eat an alkaline diet if you suffer from arthritis. Remedies are individually prescribed for you and your symptoms. Some that have been found to be useful in arthritis include rhus tox for pain and stiffness, especially on waking; bryonia for severe pain on movement and if the joints are hot and swollen; arnica if the pain is aggravated by injury, making movement difficult; ledum if pain starts in the feet and moves upward and if the joints are stiff and painful, if you feel hot inside but the limb is cold to the touch and relieved by cold compresses; ruta grav if there is pain in the tendons; and causticum if there is stiffness due to contracted tendons.

As with all the other complementary treatments it is preferable to see a qualified homoeopath who can take into account all your symptoms and prescribe the correct potency of a particular remedy, rather than trying to treat yourself.

manipulative therapies

Both these therapies involve manual manipulation of the musculo-skeletal structure of the body to relieve pain, stimulate healing and improve well-being. The techniques help to relieve pain and stiffness and improve mobility in both rheumatoid and osteoarthritis and can also be useful for treating pain arising from fibromyalgia and other soft-tissue problems.

complementary
treatments

OSTEOPATHY

Osteopathy involves manipulation of the body's structure, the skeleton, muscles, ligaments and connective tissue, in order to alleviate pain, improve mobility and restore well-being to body and mind.

Soft-tissue manipulation, using techniques similar to massage to encourage loose muscles to tighten, can relieve congestion or encourage muscle relaxation, as required.

Articulatory techniques, which involve gently stretching muscles or ligaments to relax and lengthen tight tissue, can be especially useful because in osteoarthritis shortened ligaments are responsible for limiting movement just as much as damage to the joints. Such techniques can lengthen the tissue, restoring normal function. Traction (pulling) on the ligaments, capsules and muscles over a joint can be useful for back pain or frozen shoulder.

CHIROPRACTIC

Like osteopaths, chiropractors also work on the musculo-skeletal system focusing mainly on the spine and its effects on the nervous system in the belief that damage, disease or structural changes in the spine can affect the health of the rest of the body. Chiropractic differs from osteopathic treatment in that chiropractors concentrate on specific adjustments, manipulating one joint at a time, whereas osteopaths may stretch several joints at a time. The chiropractor may use X-rays to pinpoint problems and view damage.

Treatment may involve soft tissue work, followed by manipulation. The chiropractor may use massage and 'trigger points' to loosen knots and warm up tense, painful muscles. He or she may also use ice treatments to reduce pain and swelling.

Chiropractic can be useful to ease muscular tension in arthritis which may be inhibiting movement and function, as well as easing spinal restriction which can inhibit the healing process. Treatment has to be done extremely carefully to avoid damaging the joints and tends to be more effective if begun early in the course of the disease.

diet helps

A trial of 53 people with RA carried out in 1991 showed that a naturopathic regime significantly improved symptoms. Twenty-seven sufferers stayed at a health farm and were put on a week-long fast. This was followed by a year-long special diet based on naturopathic principles. A control group of 26 sufferers were fed an ordinary diet for the course of the study. After just four weeks the special diet group showed improvements in their ability to grip and experienced less pain and fewer tender swollen joints. Blood tests showed that inflammatory activity was reduced.

ABOVE: Epsom salts are a preparation of magnesium sulphate used as a bath to relieve pain and reduce toxins.

RIGHT: A sitz bath is a form of hydrotherapy, stimulating and energizing the body.

MASSAGE

Massage is especially helpful in arthritis and rheumatism. It involves manipulating the body's soft tissues to restore health. The therapist uses his or her hands to detect and treat problems in the muscles, ligaments and tendons of the soft tissue. Regular massage is said to release emotional tension and promote physical health. Massage is also used in other therapies such as aromatherapy, Chinese medicine, Ayurvedic medicine and physiotherapy.

There are many different types of massage. Some, like shiatsu, reflexology and Chinese massage, work on pressure or reflex points. Others aim to relieve specific conditions. Massage can be either relaxing or invigorating, depending on what techniques are used. It can be especially useful for pain relief by triggering the release of endorphins, the body's own pain relievers. Massage can relax the muscles and stimulate circulation so that blood flows more freely carrying oxygen and nutrients to the joints, organs and tissues.

LEFT: Massage is a safe and enjoyable treatment that you can take as often as you like to stimulate circulation and relieve stress. You will feel the benefit straight away.

NATUROPATHY

Naturopathy is more a philosophy for living than a therapy. Naturopaths aim to maintain health by paying attention to diet and lifestyle. Disease is seen as a result of poor diet, poor elimination, injury, genetic inheritance, destructive emotions, suppressive drugs, environmental pollution or lack of exercise. Symptoms are viewed as signs that the body is trying to heal itself and rather than being suppressed may be encouraged through a range of treatments.

Diet forms the basis of good health. Foods should be as close as possible to their original state, which means choosing organic foods and eating them raw, wherever possible. Special diets, elimination diets and/or fasting may be prescribed for conditions such as arthritis and rheumatism. Fasting is said to rest the digestive system, detoxify and stimulate the metabolism. The Guelpa fast, a saline fast lasting three days, is sometimes recommended for rheumatic problems. Fasting can be effective in RA, although symptoms may recur after the fast.

Hydrotherapy, treatment using hot or cold water to alleviate pain and eliminate toxins, is also used. It can include saunas, steam, hot and cold applications, Epsom salts baths and sitz baths in which you sit alternately in baths of hot and cold water. Other techniques can include osteopathy, psychotherapy, homoeopathy, herbal treatments and exercise techniques such as yoga.

In the past most conventional doctors insisted that there was no connection between diet and arthritis. Today all this is changing as an increasing amount of research is showing that what you do or do not eat can play a major part both in prevention and treatment. In fact it is now known that **watching what you eat is one of the most positive things you can do to help your arthritis or rheumatism**. So how is food involved in arthritis? And what can you do to ensure your diet is a healthy one that will help you feel better? For a start, what you eat can affect your overall health and well-being. Eating the wrong foods can provoke stiffness, pain and swelling and this can affect your energy levels.

Second, sometimes the food you eat can actually spark off symptoms or make them worse. It has long been known that some foods may provoke gout. However research is now showing that **some rheumatoid arthritis sufferers are allergic to or intolerant of certain ingredients**. Cutting these out can bring dramatic relief from pain, swelling and stiffness in as many as one in three sufferers. Finally, researchers are discovering that **some foods can actively relieve the symptoms of arthritis and prevent them from getting worse**.

achieving a healthy balance

The first and most important thing you can do to help your arthritis is to eat a healthy diet. This will boost the health of your immune system as well as providing you with the energy you need to fight the disease process. Staying a healthy weight is especially important for anyone with joint problems as excess pounds place an increased strain on weight-bearing joints such as the back, hips, knees, ankles and feet.

So what is a healthy diet? Nutritionists and health experts generally define it as a diet that provides all the nutrients your body needs to carry out its everyday functions and to maintain a healthy weight. The best way to achieve this is to eat a varied diet. Rather than setting rigid rules about what you should and should not eat most experts today suggest thinking of your diet in terms of a plate of different foods, to guide you in what you should eat.

UNREFINED CARBOHYDRATES

The biggest portion on your plate should be unrefined carbohydrates, whole-grain starchy foods such as bread, cereals, pasta, rice, couscous and other grains. These are the foods that give your body sustained energy and fill you up so that you are not tempted to gorge on fatty, unhealthy foods. Such foods are also a good source of vitamins, minerals and fibre. When you have a chronic illness you need energy both to go about your everyday life and to help your body fight your illness. Experts recommend that you consume six or more servings of carbohdyrates a day. Unrefined starchy foods are best for health because they fill you up and keep energy levels more even.

FRUIT AND VEGETABLES

The next largest portion on the plate should be fruit and vegetables, which provide vitamins, minerals and fibre. Of particular importance are the anti-oxidant vitamins and minerals, vitamins C, E, beta carotene (which is converted into vitamin A in the body) and selenium, a trace mineral found in the soil. An increasing amount of research is being done into other nutrients found in vegetable and plant foods known as phytonutrients (plant nutrients) which actively help to prevent disease and combat symptoms. You should aim to eat at least five servings of fruit and vegetables a day. Organic fruit and vegetables are best, if you can afford them, because no pesticides and chemicals are used in their production.

BELOW: Starchy foods, such as breads, should generally make up the largest portion of the diet as they provide energy, vitamins, minerals and fibre.

BOTTOM: Vegetables are the best sources of many vitamins. Avoid overcooking them as many nutrients are destroyed by heat or will leech away in the cooking water.

PROTEIN FOODS

The next biggest portion on the plate should include protein foods needed for repair and maintenance and to maintain a healthy immune system. These include meat, poultry, game, fish, eggs, dairy products and pulses such as grains, nuts and seeds. You need around 1g of protein per kilogram (2¼lb) of your body weight every day.

Proteins in the diet are broken down by enzymes during digestion into amino acids, which are absorbed into the blood stream. These are used to repair muscles and other tissues and to build a strong and active immune system.

ABOVE: Nuts are a good source of protein.

FATS, OILS AND SUGARY FOODS

Fats, oils and sugary foods should form the smallest portion on your plate. However the body does need some fats and oils and it has recently been found that certain fats and oils, known as omega-3 and omega-6 fatty acids, can help control inflammation in people with arthritis. The problem is that the typical western diet provides too many of the wrong sorts of fats.

There are two main types of fat: saturated and unsaturated fats. Saturated fats derive mainly from animal products such as fatty meat, butter, lard, full fat milk, cheese and yogurt. Hard margarines and products such as cakes and biscuits contain a form of saturated fat known as trans-fatty acids that harm the body by triggering the production of free radicals, rogue molecules that can damage the body's cells. It is very important not to eat too many of these kinds of fats, as they are linked to obesity, high levels of blood cholesterol and furring of the arteries.

The other type of fats are unsaturated fats, found mainly in vegetables, nuts and seeds and in oily fish. Oily fish such as salmon, trout, herring and mackerel are a rich source of omega-3 fatty acids that can be especially important for people with arthritis (see page 70), while seeds such as sunflower seeds, linseeds and oily fruit such as olives are good sources of omega-6 fatty acids.

In practice this means that you should cut down on animal fats and keep fatty, sugary foods such as sweets, biscuits and cakes and sweet drinks for the occasional treat and increase your intake of foods containing healthy fats.

fat sense

→ **Spread butter more thinly or replace it with a soft margarine or a low-fat spread made from unsaturated fats.**

→ **Switch to skimmed or semi-skimmed milk.**

→ **Choose lean cuts of meat and trim off the excess fat.**

→ **Watch how you cook, for example, grill rather than fry.**

→ **Use liquid vegetable oils such as sunflower, safflower and olive rather than hard fats for cooking.**

→ **Read food labels and avoid products that are high in fat, especially saturates.**

→ **If you are not a vegetarian, replace meat with nuts and oily fish for protein on some days.**

→ **Avoid foods with hidden fats such as biscuits, cakes, pastries and savoury snacks.**

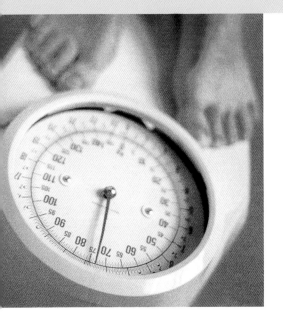

eating for a healthy weight

Maintaining a healthy weight is especially important for people with arthritis, especially osteoarthritis, where excess weight can make pain worse. Because of the way joints are constructed the pressure in knee and hip joints is equivalent to four times your body weight. So being just half a stone overweight will put 11kg (28lb) of extra pressure on your knee and hip joints. A loss of just 5–10 per cent of your body weight can reduce pain, increase mobility, increase energy, reduce fatigue and improve your self-esteem. Being the right weight for your height will also make it easier for you to exercise.

To find your ideal weight you need to calculate something the experts call your body mass index or BMI. This is done by dividing your weight in kilos by your height in metres squared. Ideally your BMI should be between 20 and 25.

To lose weight you have to consume less energy than you expend. The best way to make sure you get all the food you need is to eat a varied diet.

It is vital if you are cutting calories that you make sure you keep up your nutrient intake, so it's especially important to make nutritious food choices. The amount you need to consume to maintain health and lose weight will depend on your current weight. You can buy calorie counters to keep a check on your calorie intake but many people find it is more helpful to attend a slimming club where they have the support of other people who are also trying to lose weight. The only true way to lose weight and to keep it off is to change your eating habits for good. This is why it is best to aim for a slow, steady weight loss (about 500g–1kg/1–2lb per week) that you can maintain once you have lost the excess rather than going in for crash diets, which usually result in piling the pounds back on once the diet is finished and you return to your normal pattern of eating.

dieting tips

→ **Eat plenty of fruit and vegetables.**

→ **Cut down on fatty foods as they are the highest in calories.**

→ **Experiment with herbs and spices for flavouring rather than lashings of cream and butter.**

→ **Watch your portion sizes.**

→ **Watch your alcohol intake. Alcohol is high in calories and low in nutrients. It also increases your appetite. Stick to safe drinking limits.**

→ **Drink plenty of water.**

→ **Stock up on healthy, low-fat foods and throw out the biscuits and cakes.**

→ **Aim to have three small meals a day plus a couple of snacks so you don't feel deprived.**

→ **Enjoy what you eat.**

→ **Stay active. Muscle burns more calories than fat even when you are at rest, so by getting fitter you will burn up more calories.**

food allergies and intolerances

An increasing amount of reputable research is now showing that for some people who develop rheumatoid arthritis and other types of inflammatory arthritis and rheumatism, an allergy or intolerance to particular foods can be a contributing factor. Such foods seem to trigger an immune reaction in the body which causes inflammation and swelling. Studies have shown that cutting out these foods can significantly reduce symptoms such as pain, swelling and stiffness and in some cases can even cut out the need to take drugs.

Doctors have yet to pinpoint the exact mechanism by which certain foods trigger the inflammatory process and more research is needed, but in the meantime there are things you can do to help yourself.

identifying and avoiding the suspects

To find out whether food is a factor in your arthritis requires some patient detective work. The most usual culprits include common foods such as corn, wheat, cow's milk and dairy products, beef, pork and preserved meats like bacon, peanuts, tomatoes, chocolate and citrus fruit. However it can be extremely difficult to decide which of these foods are causing you problems for several reasons. First, you are likely to be sensitive to several different common foods. Second, reactions can take hours or even days before symptoms are experienced and they can last for days. And third, the suspects can be foods that you have eaten for years without having any problems. For this reason eliminating a single food at a time from your diet will rarely help detect the culprits. To do so you will need to cut out all the suspects for a period of one to three weeks by going on an exclusion diet, which includes only foods that are very unlikely to cause symptoms. If food is the problem you are likely to feel worse at first as you 'withdraw' from the suspect foods. However you should then begin to see an improvement as symptoms disappear.

You can then start to re-introduce foods one by one to see if they cause a reaction. This will identify the foods to which you personally react, allowing you to devise a personally tailored diet that eliminates the suspect foods.

The instructions that follow will help you, but because an elimination diet can be dangerous for some people it is wise to consult your doctor or a qualified nutritionist before you begin so that a suitable diet can be devised for you.

allergy or intolerance?

Allergies occur when the body encounters foods or other substances that it regards as foreign and potentially harmful. An allergy is a very specific response on the part of the body's immune system. The body responds to the threat by releasing antibodies into the blood stream to fight off the invader. Allergic reactions to food may affect any part of the body including the joints. Various tests can be done to identify these antibodies. Where there is an adverse reaction to food but tests for antibodies are negative the term food intolerance or food sensitivity is used. Intriguingly people are most often intolerant of foods which they eat on a regular basis, enjoy very much or crave.

BELOW: Chocolate is one of the most common triggers of food intolerances.

identifying and avoiding the suspects

1

KEEP A DIARY

The first step is to keep a detailed record of what you eat and how it affects your arthritis. List everything you eat and also list symptoms such as joint pains, stiffness and fatigue and how long they last. As well as noting joint symptoms keep a record of any other unusual symptoms or possible reactions, such as headaches and migraines, rashes and digestive upsets. You may begin to see a pattern emerge, but if you don't there is no need to worry, you can refer to the diary later on when you are testing individual foods.

2

THE EXCLUSION PHASE

During this phase you exclude most common foods and foods that you eat regularly (see page 67) and eat only foods that are unlikely to cause symptoms. Continue to keep your diary noting all symptoms including joint pains and stiffness as well as symptoms not associated with your arthritis such as headaches, fatigue, backache, muscle aches and pains, catarrh and swollen ankles. This phase can be quite tough as not only is your diet restricted but you are quite likely to feel worse initially as you withdraw from the culprits. Bear in mind that this is actually a positive sign which indicates that food is a factor in your arthritis. Any withdrawal symptoms will usually settle down after six or seven days.

3

THE RE-INTRODUCTION PHASE

During this phase you re-introduce foods one by one, leaving at least five hours between reintroducing each food so that you can see which ones cause symptoms. If you have not experienced a reaction within five hours it is safe to assume that that particular food is not a culprit and you can add it to your personal diet. It is best to leave re-introducing the most common culprits (see chart opposite) until last.

If you experience symptoms first thing in the morning they will have been sparked by foods you ate at your evening meal the night before. If you do experience symptoms, wait until they disappear before re-introducing more foods, and stick to foods that do not produce symptoms.

4

DEVISING YOUR DIET

Now you will have a list of foods that your body can tolerate and a list of those which cause your problems and which you should therefore eliminate. You can use this list to create a balanced diet which includes all the nutrients you need while omitting foods that cause you to develop symptoms. Bear in mind the rules for healthy eating outlined at the beginning of this chapter and make sure that you eat a varied diet.

FOODS TO AVOID

Meat and meat products: beef, pork, bacon, salami and other preserved meats

Fish: most fish and shellfish including smoked fish

Vegetables: potatoes, onions and sweetcorn

Cereals: wheat, oats, barley, rye and corn (maize)

Fruit: most fruits especially citrus fruits and their juices

Dairy produce: cow's milk, butter, cheese and eggs

Oils and fats: corn, soya and vegetable oils and margarines

Other: nuts and nut butters, tea, coffee, squashes, alcohol, tap water, chocolate, yeast, any food containing additives, sugar, honey, spices, vinegar, **toothpaste** (which may contain cornstarch)

FOODS TO INCLUDE

Lamb, turkey, rabbit

Trout

Carrots, sweet potatoes, spinach, celery, leeks, parsnips and swedes

White rice, sago, millet, buckwheat, and rice cakes

Fruit that you do not normally eat

Sunflower, safflower and olive oil

Herbal teas, filtered and bottled water

the deadly nightshades?

Many complementary practitioners believe that plants belonging to the nightshade (solanaceae) family can trigger arthritis. They include tomatoes, potatoes, aubergines and peppers, and spices made from peppers and chillies such as paprika, chilli powder and cayenne. Tobacco also comes from this family. Avoiding these foods is said to bring remission in symptoms of rheumatoid arthritis, osteoarthritis, SLE, ankylosing spondylitis, gout, bursitis and tendinitis, although it can take as long as six months for an improvement. Some practitioners argue that the benefit derived is related to an intolerance to these foods rather than the specific action of nightshades.

green-lipped mussels

Extracts of green-lipped mussels, a type of mussel native to New Zealand, are said to be helpful in improving osteoarthritis. Although the results are not conclusive research is promising.

spice it up

Many nutritional therapists use turmeric, the yellow spice used in curries, to help ease the pain of inflammatory arthritis. Turmeric contains an ingredient called curcumin, which has anti-inflammatory action. It also has anti-oxidant properties.

BELOW: Oily fish are rich in omega-3 fatty acids, which have an anti-inflammatory effect on the joints.

oils to quell inflammation

A great deal of scientific evidence is building up to show that fish oils can be helpful in reducing pain, inflammation and swelling in some types of arthritis (most notably rheumatoid arthritis, gout, psoriatic arthritis and osteoarthritis in which the joints are inflamed). The oils concerned contain nutrients called essential fatty acids, which the body is unable to manufacture itself and which must be derived from food. Oily fish such as salmon, trout, herrings, mackerel, pilchards and halibut are rich in nutrients called omega-3 fatty acids, which have been found to have anti-inflammatory effects on the joints.

You should aim to include fresh or smoked oily fish in your diet two or three times a week. If you don't like oily fish you can take the oils in capsule or liquid form. Other good sources of omega-3 fatty acids are walnuts, chestnuts, tofu and wild greens, such as purslane and sorrel. Because certain fats in oily fish can cause free radical damage it's advisable to make sure you include in your diet foods containing the anti-oxidant vitamin E, found in foods such as nuts, seeds, sweet potato, avocado and nut and seed oils and margarines, which will buffer any adverse effects.

Because fish oils can affect the blood's ability to clot, you should consult your doctor before taking a fish oil supplement if you have any illness affecting blood clotting, a family history of stroke, are taking anti-coagulant drugs or suffer from any other chronic illness. People with SLE and Raynaud's syndrome should avoid fish oils. Omega-3 oils have also been found to cause steep rises in blood sugar and a drop in insulin, so should be avoided by people with diabetes.

Other beneficial fats and oils include olive oil and oils such as evening primrose, borage and blackcurrant. They are rich sources of the fatty acid, gamma linolenic acid (GLA).

nutrient deficiencies and food supplements

Although few of us have gross nutrient deficiencies many of us are actually undernourished. Even small shortages of vitamins, minerals and trace elements can be enough to reduce the body's ability to function as it should. At first this may cause niggling symptoms such as colds, skin problems and fatigue, that are more a nuisance than serious. However over time these deficiencies can lead to full-scale and long-term diseases.

The problem is that although supermarkets are bursting with food, the food we eat is not as nutritious as it could be. Intensive farming, the use of pesticides, preservatives, additives and hormones, mean that food is robbed of nutrients. The use of factory farming means that the soil in which our food is grown is often depleted of minerals and the resulting crops are not as nutritious as organic varieties. Meanwhile the increased processing of food and the methods used by manufacturers to make food last longer rob food of nutrients. The preservatives can in themselves be responsible for setting up allergies.

At the same time, the way we live our lives and factors such as alcohol, smoking, the contraceptive pill and other pharmaceutical drugs (including steroids used to treat certain types of arthritis), stress and environmental pollution can cause malabsorption, in which the body doesn't absorb as many nutrients as it should.

protecting against free radical damage

Free radicals are unstable molecules that the body produces as a natural defence against disease. However sometimes the body overproduces free radicals and this in turn can provoke disease. This is thought to be a major factor in starting the disease process in osteoarthritis. Research has shown that free radicals may be involved in triggering the production of the rheumatoid factor, an antibody found in people with rheumatoid arthritis. Free radicals can be triggered by cigarette smoking, sunlight, illness, pollution and stress. Substances found in food can help ward off attack by free radicals and boost your body's defenses against cell damage. Recent research has shown that anti-oxidant vitamins, minerals and other substances known as phytochemicals found in food mop up free radicals and prevent them from damaging the cells.

Of particular importance are anti-oxidant vitamins, vitamin A, C and E. Protective minerals include iron, zinc, copper, manganese and selenium. Bioflavonoids, phytochemicals found in foods such as green vegetables, the skins of fruit, tea, coffee and wine; and carotenoids, phytochemicals found in red and orange fruit and vegetables, also have a protective action.

Researchers have also found that many people with rheumatoid and osteoarthritis are short of certain vitamins and minerals. These include the B vitamins, vitamin B6 (pyridoxine) and vitamin B5 (pantothenate), folic acid (another type of B vitamin), vitamin E, magnesium and zinc.

CHAPTER CHECKLIST

Step up your intake of fresh fruit and vegetables, rich in anti-oxidant vitamins and minerals.

Eat oily fish three times a week or consider taking a fish oil supplement.

Include plenty of nuts and seeds, good sources of omega-6 essential fatty acids, in your diet.

Make sure you get plenty of calcium-containing foods.

Try to identify any food intolerances or sensitivities.

Lose weight if you need to do so.

Take a good multi-vitamin and mineral supplement.

Check the drugs you are taking to see whether they deplete your body of any nutrients and then make sure you eat foods that contain that nutrient, or consider taking a supplement.

Ask your doctor or nutritional adviser about taking a B complex vitamin supplement.

If you want to consider specific supplements consult a qualified nutritionist.

ABOVE: Walnuts are a rich source of magnesium, iron, vitamin E, B vitamins, folic acid and copper, all nutrients thought to reduce arthritis.

supplementary benefits

Because arthritis and rheumatism can lead to poor appetite it may be that you are not getting enough of certain nutrients from your diet alone. Taking a good multi-vitamin and mineral supplement can help ensure you get all the nutrients you need. What is more the uptake of certain vitamins may be damaged by some drugs used to treat arthritis. For example the action of B complex vitamins may be blocked by certain drugs. You should ask your doctor about taking a supplement or consult a qualified nutritional expert. There is also a lot of ongoing research into the role of certain nutrient supplements. These include zinc, copper, B vitamins and two amino acids called glucosamine and chondroitin. Because taking supplements can disturb the balance of other nutrients in your body it is wise to get advice from a qualified nutritionist, rather than dosing yourself willy nilly.

NUTRIENT	GOOD SOURCES	WAYS IT CAN HELP
Beta carotene (converted in the body to vitamin A)	Red, yellow and green fruit and vegetables such as apricots, squash and carrots.	Anti-oxidant, protects against free radical damage. Also needed for healthy cell division and growth.
Vitamin C	Found in most fruit and vegetables. Rich sources include strawberries, blackcurrants, guavas and kiwi fruit.	Vital for production of collagen, a component of cartilage, and other tissues. Antioxidant, protects against free radical damage.
Vitamin E	Nuts and seeds	Antioxidant, protects against oxidation of polyunsaturated fats in cell membranes. Especially important if your diet is rich in fish and other polyunsaturated fats.
B complex vitamins		
Vitamin B5 (pantothenic acid)	Wholemeal bread, nuts, chestnuts and dried fruits.	May help ease pain and morning stiffness.
Vitamin B6 (pyridoxine)	Offal, poultry, fish, eggs, brown rice, nuts, soya beans and wholegrains.	Helps immune and nervous system function. Helpful in carpal tunnel syndrome.
Folic acid	Green leafy vegetables, eggs, nuts, yeast extract and wholegrains.	May be low in people taking methotrexate. Helps reduce toxicity of drug.
Vitamin D	Margarine, oily fish, egg yolks, exposure to sunlight.	Helps the body utilize calcium, which is vital for strong bones and to prevent osteoporosis.
Boron	Grapes, plums, dried fruit, green leafy vegetables and avocado.	May help improve symptoms of osteoarthritis. May also reduce losses of calcium and magnesium so helping protect against osteoporosis.
Magnesium	Green vegetables, wheat, whole oats, walnuts almonds, rice, sorrel, okra, cashews, cabbage and dill.	Shortage of magnesium may increase levels of inflammatory cells. Magnesium is needed to aid absorption of calcium from food to create strong bones. Shortage may be linked to osteoporosis.

NUTRIENT	GOOD SOURCES	WAYS IT CAN HELP
Zinc	Apricots, peaches, nectarines, oysters, wheatgerm, cocoa, mustard seeds, Brewer's yeast, eggs and pumpkin seeds.	People with RA sometimes have low levels of zinc. In psoriatic arthritis zinc can help relieve pain, stiffness and swelling. Also needed for strong bones.
Iron	Wheat, rice, Brazil nuts, green leafy vegetables, apples, grapes, walnuts, dill, dandelion leaves, pumpkin, squash and plums.	Needed for healthy blood. Shortage can lead to anaemia and fatigue. People with RA are prone to anaemia.
Calcium	Sesame seeds, seaweeds, kale, turnips, almonds, soya beans, dandelion leaves, hazelnuts, horseradish, honey, salmon, milk, cheese and dairy products.	Essential for strong bones to help prevent osteoporosis.
Copper	Peaches, turnips, lentils, shellfish and nuts.	Can help prevent osteoporosis. A constituent of an anti-oxidant enzyme in some inflammatory reactions. Both copper deficiency and copper overload have been linked to RA.
Manganese	Apples, peaches, rye, turnips, tea, wholemeal bread and avocado.	Involved in formation of cartilage. Shortage of manganese causes joint pain. Needed for normal bone structure and may help prevent osteoporosis.
Selenium	Wheatgerm, bran, onions, broccoli, shellfish and tuna.	Important anti-oxidant. Low levels found in RA and OA. May help prevent RA when combined with Carotenoids and vitamin E. Shortage linked to arthralgia, joint pain and muscle pain.

vital vitamins and minerals

Everyone should aim to eat a healthy, nutritious diet, but this is an especially important goal if you have rheumatism or arthritis, because **what you eat can help you fight your condition**.

You'll find **recipes that are high in the anti-oxidant vitamins and minerals** which help to combat the free-radical damage that is thought to play a part in triggering several different types of arthritis and rheumatism. There is also **a selection of recipes using oily fish**, which can be helpful for their anti-inflammatory properties, to encourage you to start including more omega-3 fatty acids in your diet.

Because staying a healthy weight is so important in reducing stress on the joints, **each recipe is calorie counted and has a breakdown of the nutrients it contains**. Many are **quick and simple to prepare**, which is vital for those days when you are not feeling well and want something easy to make.

Use the recipes when you've identified the foods that cause you problems. Once you've got a few ideas you can adapt other recipes to **exclude the foods that make your symptoms worse**.

mexican soup with avocado salsa

Serves 6 – Preparation time: 30 minutes – Cooking time: 45 minutes

Per serving – Energy: 199 kcals / 836 kJ · Protein: 8 g · Carbohydrate: 24 g · Fat: 9 g · Fibre: 7 g

✔ alcohol free
citrus free
✔ dairy free
gluten free
wheat free

2	**tablespoons sunflower oil**
1	**large onion, chopped**
2	**garlic cloves, crushed**
2	**teaspoons ground coriander**
1	**teaspoon ground cumin**
1	**red pepper, cored, deseeded and diced**
3	**red chillies, deseeded and sliced**
400 g	**(13 oz) can red kidney beans, drained**
750 ml	**(1¼ pints) tomato juice**
½	**tablespoon chilli sauce**
25 g	**(1 oz) tortilla corn chips, crushed**
	salt
	pepper
	coriander sprigs, to garnish

Avocado Salsa:

1	**small ripe avocado**
4	**spring onions, finely chopped**
1	**tablespoon lemon juice**
1	**tablespoon chopped coriander**

1 Heat the oil in a large, heavy-based saucepan, add the onion, garlic, spices, red pepper and two-thirds of the chillies and fry gently for 10 minutes. Add the kidney beans, tomato juice and chilli sauce and bring to the boil then cover and simmer gently for 30 minutes.

2 Meanwhile, make the avocado salsa. Peel, stone and finely dice the avocado, put it into a bowl and combine with the spring onions, lemon juice and coriander. Season to taste with salt and pepper, cover with clingfilm and set aside.

3 Process the soup in a food processor or blender with the crushed tortilla chips. Return the soup to a clean saucepan, season to taste and heat through. Serve the soup at once with the avocado salsa, garnished with the reserved chilli slices and some coriander sprigs.

borscht

Serves 6 – Preparation time: 10 minutes – Cooking time: 1 hour

Per serving – Energy: 64 kcals / 269 kJ · Protein: 4 g · Carbohydrate: 13 g · Fat: 1 g · Fibre: 3 g

500 g	(1 lb) raw beetroot
2	carrots
1	onion
1.2	litres (2 pints) beef stock
1	bay leaf
	salt
	pepper
150 ml	(¹/₄ pint) natural yogurt, to garnish

1 Grate or finely chop the beetroot. Finely chop 1 of the carrots and the onion. Grate the second carrot. Put the vegetables, stock and bay leaf into a saucepan and season with salt and pepper. Bring to the boil then reduce the heat and simmer for 1 hour. Taste the soup and adjust the seasoning, if necessary.

2 Pour the borscht into warmed individual soup bowls and garnish each serving with a spoonful of yogurt.

alcohol free ✔
citrus free ✔
dairy free
gluten free ✔
wheat free ✔

spring vegetable broth

Serves 4 – Preparation time: 10 minutes – Cooking time: 40 minutes

Per serving – Energy: 88 kcals / 370 kJ · Protein: 3 g · Carbohydrate: 14 g · Fat: 2 g · Fibre: 4 g

2	teaspoons olive oil
2	celery sticks with their leaves, chopped
2	leeks, chopped
1	carrot, finely diced
50 g	(2 oz) pearl barley
1.2	litres (2 pints) vegetable stock
125 g	(4 oz) mangetout, diagonally sliced
	salt
	pepper

1 Heat the oil in a saucepan and add the chopped celery and leaves, leeks and carrot. Cook over a moderate heat for 10 minutes.

2 Stir in the pearl barley and stock, season to taste with salt and pepper and simmer for 20 minutes. Add the mangetout and simmer for a further 10 minutes. Ladle into warmed bowls and serve.

alcohol free ✔
citrus free ✔
dairy free ✔
gluten free ✔
wheat free ✔

gazpacho

Serves 6 – Preparation time: 15 minutes, plus chilling

Per serving – Energy: 118 kcals / 493 kJ · Protein: 2 g · Carbohydrate: 10 g · Fat: 8 g · Fibre: 1 g

✔ alcohol free
  citrus free
✔ dairy free
✔ gluten free
✔ wheat free

1	garlic clove, halved
1	litre (1³/₄ pints) tomato juice
3	tablespoons olive oil
2	tablespoons lemon juice
1	tablespoon lime juice
2	teaspoons sugar
150 g	(5 oz) cucumber, peeled and diced
75 g	(3 oz) mild red onion or spring onion, chopped
150 g	(5 oz) red pepper, cored, deseeded and diced
75 g	(3 oz) avocado, stoned, peeled and diced
2	tablespoons chopped mixed herbs, such as parsley, chives, basil and marjoram
	salt
	pepper
	ice cubes, to serve

1 Rub the cut surfaces of the garlic over the bottom and sides of a mixing bowl then discard the garlic. Pour the tomato juice into the bowl and add the oil, lemon and lime juices, sugar and salt and pepper to taste. Lightly beat together, then cover and chill for at least 1 hour.

2 Beat the soup base again, then add the cucumber, onion, red pepper, avocado and herbs and stir gently. Alternatively serve the diced ingredients in separate bowls so that the diners can help themselves.

3 Put ice cubes into individual soup bowls and add the soup.

butternut squash and rosemary soup

Serves 4 – Preparation time: 15 minutes – Cooking time: about 1¹/₄ hours

Per serving – Energy: 173 kcals / 737 kJ · Protein: 11 g · Carbohydrate: 33 g · Fat: 1 g · Fibre: 5 g

✔ alcohol free
✔ citrus free
✔ dairy free
✔ gluten free
✔ wheat free

1	butternut squash
4	rosemary sprigs, plus extra to garnish
150 g	(5 oz) red lentils, washed
1	onion, finely chopped
900 ml	(1¹/₂ pints) vegetable stock
	salt
	pepper

1 Halve the squash and, using a spoon, scoop out the seeds and fibrous flesh. Cut the squash into smaller chunks and place them in a roasting tin. Sprinkle over the rosemary and season with salt and pepper. Roast in a preheated oven at 200°C (400°F), Gas Mark 6 for 45 minutes.

2 Meanwhile, place the lentils in a saucepan. Cover with water, bring to the boil and boil rapidly for 10 minutes. Strain, then return the lentils to a clean saucepan with the onion and stock and simmer for 5 minutes. Season to taste.

3 Remove the squash from the oven and scoop out the flesh, mash it with a fork and add to the soup. Simmer for 25 minutes then ladle into warmed bowls. Garnish with more rosemary before serving.

carrot and coriander pâté

Serves 4 – Preparation time: 10 minutes, plus chilling – Cooking time: 40 minutes
Per serving – Energy: 87 kcals / 362 kJ · Protein: 3 g · Carbohydrate: 14 g · Fat: 3 g · Fibre: 3 g

500 g **(1 lb) carrots, grated**
1 **tablespoon ground coriander**
175 ml **(6 fl oz) freshly squeezed orange juice**
300 ml **(1/2 pint) water**
50 g **(2 oz) medium-fat soft cheese**
30 g **(1 1/4 oz) coriander leaves, plus extra**
to garnish
salt
pepper
crusty bread, to serve

1 Place the carrot in a pan with the ground coriander, orange juice and water. Cover with a lid and simmer for 40 minutes until the carrots are cooked. Leave to cool.

2 Transfer the carrot mixture to a food processor or blender with a little of the cooking liquid, add the soft cheese and coriander leaves and blend until smooth. Season to taste with salt and pepper and blend again. Spoon into small dishes, garnish with coriander sprigs, cover and chill. Serve with crusty bread.

alcohol free ✔
citrus free
dairy free
gluten free ✔
wheat free ✔

VARIATION

chickpea and carrot pâté

Preparation time: 10 minutes, plus chilling
Cooking time: 40 minutes
Per serving – Energy: 164 kcals /690 KJ · Protein: 7 g
Carbohydrate: 25 g · Fat: 4 g · Fibre: 3 g

alcohol free ✔
citrus free
dairy free
gluten free ✔
wheat free ✔

1 Follow the main recipe, replacing the coriander leaves with 275 g (9 oz) drained canned chickpeas. Blend until smooth. Spoon into small dishes and chill until ready to serve.

chickpea, spinach and pasta soup

Serves 6 – Preparation time: 15 minutes – Cooking time: 45 minutes

Per serving – Energy: 248 kcals / 1046 kJ · Protein: 12 g · Carbohydrate: 34 g · Fat: 8 g · Fibre: 6 g

✔ alcohol free
✔ citrus free
  dairy free
  gluten free
  wheat free

6	**tablespoons extra virgin olive oil**
2	**garlic cloves, crushed**
1	**onion, chopped**
1	**tablespoon chopped rosemary**
2 x	**425 g (14 oz) cans chickpeas**
1.2	**litres (2 pints) vegetable stock**
75 g	**(3 oz) small pasta shapes**
4	**thick slices of day-old white bread**
125 g	**(4 oz) spinach leaves, shredded**
	salt
	pepper

To Serve:
freshly grated nutmeg
freshly grated Parmesan cheese

1 Heat 2 tablespoons of the oil in a large saucepan and fry the garlic, onion and rosemary for 5 minutes until softened. Add the chickpeas with their liquid and the stock, bring to the boil, cover and simmer for 30 minutes. Add the pasta, return to the boil and simmer for 6–8 minutes.

2 Meanwhile, make the croûtons. Remove the crusts from the bread and cut the bread into cubes. Heat the remaining olive oil in a frying pan. When the oil is hot add the bread and stir-fry for 2–3 minutes until the bread cubes are golden and crisp. Remove the croûtons from the pan with a slotted spoon and drain thoroughly on kitchen paper.

3 Stir the spinach into the soup and continue cooking for a further 5 minutes until both the pasta and spinach are tender. Season to taste and serve at once topped with nutmeg, croûtons and grated Parmesan.

burmese noodle soup with marinated chicken

Serves 6 – Preparation time: 20 minutes, plus standing – Cooking time: about 35 minutes

Per serving – Energy: 573 kcals / 2412 kJ · Protein: 33 g · Carbohydrate: 71 g · Fat: 20 g · Fibre: 5 g

300 g	(10 oz) boneless, skinless chicken breasts
1	teaspoon turmeric
2	teaspoons salt
3	tablespoons peanuts, skinned
2	lemon grass stalks
3	tablespoons white long-grain rice
2	tablespoons vegetable oil
1	onion, chopped
3	garlic cloves, crushed
5	cm (2 inch) piece of fresh root ginger, peeled and finely chopped
¹/₄	teaspoon paprika
2	red bird's eye chillies, chopped
2–3	tablespoons Thai fish sauce
900 ml	(1¹/₂ pints) water
250 g	(8 oz) wheat noodles

To Serve:

3	hard-boiled eggs, halved
2	tablespoons chopped coriander leaves
3	spring onions, finely chopped
	crushed dried chilli

1 Cut the chicken breasts into 2.5 cm (1 inch) cubes. Mix the turmeric with the salt and rub the mixture into the chicken. Leave to stand for 30 minutes.

2 Meanwhile, toast the peanuts in a dry frying pan, stirring continuously, until golden. Leave to cool. Bruise the lemon grass with the side of a rolling pin to release the flavour. Finely crush the roasted peanuts in a food processor or using a pestle and mortar. Heat a dry frying pan and toast the rice until golden brown, then crush it to a fine powder in a food processor or spice grinder.

3 Heat the oil in a large saucepan and fry the onion until just softened. Add the marinated chicken with the garlic, ginger, lemon grass, paprika and chillies. Add the fish sauce and water and bring to the boil.

4 Reduce the heat to a simmer. Mix together the crushed peanuts and ground rice and add to the pan. Simmer for about 10–15 minutes, or until the chicken has cooked through and the broth thickened slightly.

5 Meanwhile, bring a pan of water to the boil, add the wheat noodles and cook for 3–4 minutes, or until just done. Drain and refresh with cold water then divide them between large warmed soup bowls.

6 Ladle the chicken soup over the noodles and serve topped with the hard-boiled eggs, chopped coriander and spring onions. Add an extra splash of fish sauce and a sprinkling of crushed dried chilli, to taste. Eat the soup with a spoon and fork.

alcohol free	✔
citrus free	✔
dairy free	✔
gluten free	
wheat free	

griddled salmon fillets with pesto and lemon butter rice

Serves 4 – Preparation time: 15 minutes – Cooking time: about 20 minutes

Per serving – Energy: 544 kcals / 2265 kJ · Protein: 33 g · Carbohydrate: 17 g · Fat: 39 g · Fibre: 0 g

✔ alcohol free
✔ citrus free
dairy free
✔ gluten free
✔ wheat free

75 g **(3 oz) long-grain rice**
grated rind and juice of 1 lemon
4 x **150 g (5 oz) salmon fillets**
50 g **(2 oz) butter**
basil leaves, to garnish (optional)

Pesto:
1 **garlic clove, chopped**
15 g **(¹/₂ oz) pine nuts**
15 g **(¹/₂ oz) basil leaves**
3 **tablespoons extra virgin olive oil**
1 **tablespoon freshly grated**
  Parmesan cheese
sea salt flakes
pepper

1 Bring a large saucepan of water to the boil. Add the rice and the lemon rind, and return to the boil. Simmer gently for 10–12 minutes, or according to the packet instructions, until the rice is cooked.

2 Meanwhile, to make the pesto, place all the ingredients in a food processor or blender and process until smooth.

3 Heat a griddle pan or nonstick frying pan. Remove any remaining bones from the salmon with a pair of tweezers, and pat dry on kitchen paper. Place the fillets on the hot griddle, skin-side down, and cook for 3 minutes. Turn and cook for another 2–3 minutes until cooked through and firm to the touch.

4 Drain the rice and immediately stir in the lemon juice and butter. Season to taste. Serve the salmon fillets on a bed of rice with the pesto sauce. Garnish with basil leaves, if liked.

tarragon-infused sea bass fillets

Serves 4 – Preparation time: 5 minutes – Cooking time: 6 minutes

Per serving – Energy: 225 kcals / 944 kJ · Protein: 34 g · Carbohydrate: 0 g · Fat: 10 g · Fibre: 0 g

4 x 175 g (6 oz) sea bass fillets
1 large bunch of tarragon
2 tablespoons olive oil
4 tablespoons lemon juice
sea salt flakes
pepper

1 Heat a griddle pan or nonstick frying pan, add the sea bass, skin-side down, and cook for 3 minutes. Place a quarter of the tarragon on each fillet, pressing it into the fish. Turn the fish so that it is resting on the tarragon and cook for another 3 minutes.

2 To serve, drizzle the fillets with olive oil and lemon juice, and season with salt and pepper. Serve with the charred tarragon.

alcohol free	✔
citrus free	
dairy free	✔
gluten free	✔
wheat free	✔

grilled sardines with tabbouleh

Serves 4 – Preparation time: 10 minutes – Cooking time: 15 minutes

Per serving – Energy: 250 kcals / 1053 kJ · Protein: 19 g · Carbohydrate: 27 g · Fat: 8 g · Fibre: 1 g

125 g (4 oz) bulgar wheat
1 onion, finely chopped
2 ripe tomatoes, skinned and deseeded
1 tablespoon lemon juice
1 teaspoon grated lemon rind
a small handful of mint leaves
4 small sardines, gutted and boned
salt
pepper

To Garnish:
lemon wedges
salad or herb leaves

1 Bring a small saucepan of water to the boil and add the bulgar wheat. Simmer for 5 minutes, then drain and refresh under cold water. Drain again and put into a bowl. Meanwhile, dry-fry the onion for 5 minutes.

2 Add the onion, tomatoes, lemon juice and rind to the bulgar wheat. Set aside 4 mint leaves and chop the remainder. Stir the chopped mint into the bulgar wheat mixture; season well.

3 Open out each sardine and lay a mint leaf along the centre. Spoon over a little of the tabbouleh then carefully fold back the fillet to reshape the fish.

4 Cook the sardines under a preheated hot grill for 5 minutes on each side. Serve with the remaining tabbouleh, garnished with lemon wedges and a few salad or herb leaves.

alcohol free	✔
citrus free	
dairy free	✔
gluten free	
wheat free	

griddled tuna on a bed of rice noodles with ginger and soy sauce

Serves 4 – Preparation time: 15 minutes – Cooking time: about 15 minutes

Per serving – Energy: 479 kcals / 2009 kJ · Protein: 34 g · Carbohydrate: 53 g · Fat: 14 g · Fibre: 0 g

✔ alcohol free
  citrus free
✔ dairy free
✔ gluten free
✔ wheat free

1	**tablespoon grapeseed oil**
5 cm	**(2 inch) piece of fresh root ginger, peeled and finely diced**
2	**garlic cloves, chopped**
2	**shallots, finely chopped**
1	**green chilli, deseeded and finely chopped**
1	**lemon grass stalk, finely sliced**
500 g	**(1 lb) tuna fillet, in 1 piece**
250 g	**(8 oz) rice noodles**
	grated rind and juice of 1 lime
2	**tablespoons soy sauce**
2	**tablespoons sesame oil**
1	**bunch of coriander, chopped**

To Garnish:
1 **lime, cut into 4 wedges**
   coriander sprigs
   spring onion slivers

1 Heat a little grapeseed oil in a small saucepan, add the ginger, garlic, shallots, chilli and lemon grass. Heat gently until softened, but do not brown.

2 Heat a griddle pan or nonstick frying pan and add the tuna fillet. Cook for 1–2 minutes on each side over a moderate to high heat, gradually turning so that all sides have been charred. The tuna is meant to be rare, but if this is not to your liking, griddle for longer. When cooked, rest the tuna for 3 minutes.

3 Plunge the noodles into a large pan of boiling water and cook for 2 minutes, or according to the packet instructions. Drain well and return to the pan. Add the cooked ginger mixture, the lime rind and juice, soy sauce and sesame oil. Toss well, then cover and keep warm.

4 Place the lime wedges on the griddle and cook for 1 minute on each side. This will give a charred effect and warm the juice slightly. Add the chopped coriander to the rice noodles and toss well. Arrange the noodles in a large serving dish. Cut the tuna into 1 cm (½ inch) slices and arrange on top of the rice noodles. Garnish with griddled lime wedges, coriander sprigs and spring onion slivers, and serve immediately.

quick griddled scallops with sage

Serves 4 – Preparation time: 10 minutes – Cooking time: 5–7 minutes

Per serving – Energy: 192 kcals / 807 kJ · Protein: 23 g · Carbohydrate: 3 g · Fat: 10 g · Fibre: 0 g

16	**scallops**
1	**large bunch of sage leaves**
3	**tablespoons olive oil**
1	**tablespoon balsamic vinegar**
	sea salt flakes
	pepper
4	**lemon wedges, to garnish**

1 Dry the scallops thoroughly with kitchen paper.

2 Heat a griddle pan or nonstick frying pan, add the scallops and cook for 2–3 minutes on each side. Add the sage leaves and cook until just wilting.

3 Mix together the olive oil and the balsamic vinegar in a shallow dish. Remove the scallops and sage from the heat and toss well in the dressing. Season to taste and serve immediately with wedges of lemon.

alcohol free ✔
citrus free
dairy free ✔
gluten free ✔
wheat free ✔

tuna steaks with quick tomato sauce

Serves 4 – Preparation time: 5 minutes – Cooking time: 20–25 minutes

Per serving – Energy: 157 kcals / 660 kJ · Protein: 25 g · Carbohydrate: 4 g · Fat: 5 g · Fibre: 1 g

4 x	**100 g (3¹/₂ oz) tuna steaks**
	Tomato Sauce:
4	**plum tomatoes**
1	**teaspoon garlic purée**
1	**tablespoon tomato purée**
1	**tablespoon chopped parsley**
	salt
	pepper

1 Heat a griddle pan or nonstick frying pan until it is very hot and cook the tuna steaks, 2 at a time, for 3 minutes on each side. Remove from the pan and keep warm.

2 To make the tomato sauce, put all the sauce ingredients into a food processor or blender and purée for 1 minute. Transfer to a saucepan and cook, uncovered, for 10 minutes. Season and spoon over the cooked tuna.

alcohol free ✔
citrus free ✔
dairy free ✔
gluten free ✔
wheat free ✔

salmon with a chilli crust

Serves 4 – **Preparation time: 10 minutes** – **Cooking time: 8 minutes**

Per serving – Energy: 319 kcals / 1328 kJ · Protein: 33 g · Carbohydrate: 0 g · Fat: 21 g · Fibre: 0 g

✔ alcohol free
citrus free
✔ dairy free
✔ gluten free
✔ wheat free

3 **teaspoons crushed dried chilli**
8 **teaspoons sesame seeds**
1 **large bunch of parsley, chopped**
4 x **150 g (5 oz) salmon fillets, skinned**
1 **egg white, lightly beaten**
sea salt
pepper

To Serve:
1 **lime, cut into wedges**
noodles

1 Heat a nonstick frying pan. Mix together the crushed dried chilli, sesame seeds, parsley and salt and pepper and sprinkle on a plate.

2 Dip the salmon fillets in the egg white, then coat them in the chilli crust mixture, patting the mixture on to the salmon to ensure an even coating.

3 Place the salmon fillets on the hot pan and cook for 4 minutes on each side, turning them carefully with a palette knife and keeping the crust on the fish. When cooked, remove and serve with the lime quarters and noodles, if liked.

catalan mussels

Serves 4 – **Preparation time: 10 minutes** – **Cooking time: about 20 minutes**

Per serving – Energy: 126 kcals / 534 kJ · Protein: 13 g · Carbohydrate: 9 g · Fat: 5 g · Fibre: 1 g

✔ alcohol free
✔ citrus free
✔ dairy free
✔ gluten free
✔ wheat free

1 **tablespoon olive oil**
1 **onion, finely chopped**
2 **garlic cloves, crushed**
1 **red chilli, deseeded and finely chopped**
pinch of paprika
400 g **(13 oz) can chopped tomatoes**
1 kg **(2 lb) fresh mussels, scrubbed and bearded**
salt
pepper
chopped parsley, to garnish

1 Heat the oil in a large saucepan or wok. Fry the onion, garlic, chilli and paprika over a moderate heat for 5 minutes or until soft. Stir in the tomatoes and season with salt and pepper. Cover and simmer over a low heat for about 10 minutes.

2 Check the mussels. Discard any shells that remain open after you have tapped them on the work surface or any that are broken.

3 Stir the mussels into the tomato sauce, increase the temperature and cover with a lid. Cook for 5 minutes until the shells have opened. Discard any mussels that remain closed.

4 Pile the mussels into warmed serving bowls, sprinkle with chopped parsley and serve.

green marinated ginger and garlic prawns

Serves 4 – Preparation time: 20 minutes, plus marinating – Cooking time: 10 minutes

Per serving – Energy: 213 kcals / 892 kJ · Protein: 12 g · Carbohydrate: 33 g · Fat: 3 g · Fibre: 0 g

24	raw tiger prawns, peeled, heads removed and deveined
5 cm	(2 inch) piece of fresh root ginger, peeled and finely diced
4	large garlic cloves, crushed
1	green chilli, deseeded and finely chopped
1	bunch of spring onions, cut into 5 cm (2 inch) lengths
150 g	(5 oz) rice noodles
1	tablespoon sesame oil
2	tablespoons soy sauce
1	bunch of coriander, chopped grated rind and juice of 1 lime sea salt pepper

1 Place the prepared prawns in a non-metallic dish, add the ginger, garlic and chilli and mix well. Cover and leave to marinate in the refrigerator for at least 2 hours.

2 Cut the spring onion lengths into thin strips. Place them in iced water. The longer they are left and the colder the water, the curlier they will become.

3 Heat a griddle pan or nonstick frying pan. Put the prawns on the hot pan and cook for 3 minutes on each side.

4 Bring a saucepan of lightly salted water to the boil, add the rice noodles and cook for 2 minutes. Drain well, then add the sesame oil, soy sauce, coriander, lime rind and juice, and salt and pepper to taste, and toss well. Serve with the prawns and spring onion curls.

alcohol free ✔
citrus free
dairy free ✔
gluten free ✔
wheat free ✔

green-lipped mussels with garlic butter

Serves 4 – Preparation time: 10 minutes – Cooking time: 5–6 minutes

Per serving – Energy: 276 kcals / 1140 kJ · Protein: 9 g · Carbohydrate: 0 g · Fat: 27 g · Fibre: 0 g

✔ alcohol free
✔ citrus free
  dairy free
✔ gluten free
✔ wheat free

2	garlic cloves, crushed
125 g	(4 oz) butter, softened
1	bunch of parsley, chopped
24	ready-cooked green-lipped mussels
	sea salt
	pepper

To Serve:
crusty bread
green salad

Green-lipped mussels, which are usually sold ready-cooked in their half shells, are available from good fishmongers. If you are unable to find them, use ordinary small mussels but increase the quantity.

1 Heat a griddle pan or nonstick frying pan. Mix the crushed garlic into the softened butter with the parsley and salt and pepper to taste.

2 Spread the butter over the mussel halves with a palette knife then place them on the hot pan, shell side down. Cook the mussels for 5–6 minutes or until all the butter has melted. Serve with crusty bread to mop up all the juices, and a fresh green salad.

trout in coriander

Serves 4 – Preparation time: 10 minutes – Cooking time: 20 minutes

Per serving – Energy: 429 kcals / 1798 kJ · Protein: 50 g · Carbohydrate: 4 g · Fat: 24 g · Fibre: 0 g

1 kg	**(2 lb) rainbow trout fillets**
4	**tablespoons lime or lemon juice**
2	**teaspoons salt**
4	**tablespoons olive oil**
25 g	**(1 oz) fresh breadcrumbs**
1	**garlic clove, crushed**
6	**tablespoons crushed coriander leaves**
1	**teaspoon lime or lemon rind, cut into strips**
	pepper
	lime wedges, to serve

1 Rinse the fish fillets under cold running water and pat dry with kitchen paper. Rub the fish with half of the lime or lemon juice and half the salt, then place them skin-side down in a lightly oiled heavy-based frying pan.

2 Add sufficient cold water to cover the fish. Bring to the boil and simmer gently for 5 minutes, turning the fish twice during the cooking time. Drain well and place the fillets in a single layer in an ovenproof dish.

3 In another pan, heat half of the olive oil. Add the breadcrumbs, garlic, the remaining salt and 4 tablespoons of the coriander and cook gently, stirring constantly, until the crumbs are golden brown. Spread over the fish and bake in a preheated oven at 200°C (400°F), Gas Mark 6 for 7–10 minutes, until the fish flakes easily.

4 Blend the remaining lime or lemon juice and oil, and pour over the fish. Cook for another 2–3 minutes. Combine the remaining coriander with the lime or lemon rind strips and sprinkle over the fish. Season with pepper and serve hot with lime wedges.

alcohol free ✔
citrus free
dairy free ✔
gluten free
wheat free

carnival chicken with sweet potato mash

Serves 4 – Preparation time: 15–20 minutes, plus marinating – Cooking time: 20 minutes
Per serving – Energy: 315 kcals / 1330 kJ · Protein: 36 g · Carbohydrate: 26 g · Fat: 5 g · Fibre: 3 g

alcohol free
✔ citrus free
dairy free
✔ gluten free
✔ wheat free

4 x	**150 g (5 oz) boneless, skinless chicken breasts**
	flat-leaf parsley sprigs, to garnish

Marinade:
100 ml	**(3¹/₂ fl oz) sweet sherry**
1	**teaspoon Angostura bitters**
1	**tablespoon light soy sauce**
1	**tablespoon chopped fresh root ginger**
	pinch of ground cumin
	pinch of ground coriander
1	**teaspoon dried mixed herbs**
1	**small onion, finely chopped**
75 ml	**(3 fl oz) chicken stock**

Sweet Potato Mash:
2	**sweet potatoes**
2	**tablespoons very low-fat fromage frais (optional)**
	salt
	pepper

1 Place the chicken breasts in a non-metallic dish. In a bowl mix together all the marinade ingredients. Spoon over the chicken, making sure the pieces are well coated. Cover and leave to marinate in the refrigerator overnight.

2 Place the chicken breasts on a grill pan and cook under a preheated moderate grill for 20 minutes, turning them over halfway through cooking.

3 Meanwhile, boil the sweet potatoes in their skins for 20 minutes, until soft. Drain well and peel. Mash the potatoes and let them dry a little, then stir in the fromage frais, if using. Season with salt and pepper and serve with the chicken. Garnish with the parsley sprigs.

lamb casserole with roasted garlic and chilli

Serves 4 – Preparation time: 20 minutes – Cooking time: 1¹/₂–2 hours

Per serving – Energy: 596 kcals / 2503 kJ · Protein: 47 g · Carbohydrate: 43 g · Fat: 28 g · Fibre: 6 g

2	large red or green chillies
2	large garlic cloves, unpeeled
1	teaspoon coriander seeds, toasted and crushed
1	teaspoon cumin seeds, toasted and crushed
3	tablespoons oil
750 g	(1¹/₂ lb) boneless lamb, cubed
1	onion, chopped
375 g	(12 oz) cooked brown long-grain rice
125 g	(4 oz) cooked chickpeas
400 g	(13 oz) can chopped tomatoes
1	large aubergine, diced
75 g	(3 oz) green beans, chopped
450 ml	(³/₄ pint) vegetable stock
3	tablespoons chopped coriander
	salt
	pepper

To Garnish:
natural yogurt
4 red chillies

alcohol free ✔
citrus free ✔
dairy free
gluten free ✔
wheat free ✔

1 Spread the chillies and garlic on a baking sheet and roast in a preheated oven at 220°C (425°F), Gas Mark 7 for 15–20 minutes. Remove from the oven, cool slightly then remove the skins and seeds from the chilli and the skins from the garlic. Put them in a small bowl with the coriander and cumin seeds and mash to a paste.

2 Heat 1 tablespoon of the oil in a heavy-based saucepan, add the lamb and brown it evenly. Remove the lamb from the pan with a slotted spoon and set it aside.

3 Heat the remaining oil in the pan and gently fry the onion for 5 minutes. Add the chilli paste and stir-fry for another minute.

4 Return the lamb to the pan and add the rice, chickpeas, tomatoes, aubergine, beans, stock and salt and pepper to taste. Bring to the boil then cover and simmer gently for 1–1¹/₂ hours, or until tender. Stir in the coriander, and garnish with the yogurt and red chillies.

V A R I A T I O N

chicken casserole with roasted garlic and chilli

Preparation time: 20 minutes
Cooking time: 1¹/₂–2 hours
Per serving – Energy: 510 kcals / 2147 kJ · Protein: 49 g
Carbohydrate: 43 g · Fat: 17 g · Fibre: 6 g

alcohol free ✔
citrus free ✔
dairy free
gluten free ✔
wheat free ✔

1 Replace the lamb with the same quantity of cubed, boneless, skinless chicken breast and cook as in the main recipe.

marinated chicken kebabs

Serves 4 – Preparation time: 15 minutes, plus marinating – Cooking time: 15 minutes

Per serving – Energy: 517 kcals / 2155 kJ · Protein: 42 g · Carbohydrate: 9 g · Fat: 35 g · Fibre: 1 g

✔ alcohol free
citrus free
dairy free
✔ gluten free
✔ wheat free

4   boneless, skinless chicken breasts

Marinade:
4   tablespoons lime juice
1   tablespoon honey
**1   green chilli, deseeded and finely
      chopped**
2   tablespoons olive oil

Avocado Sauce:
3   tablespoons olive oil
1   tablespoon red wine vinegar
**1   large avocado, peeled,
      stoned and mashed**
**1   large tomato, skinned,
      deseeded and chopped**
2   spring onions, chopped
125 ml (4 fl oz) soured cream

To Garnish:
lime rind strips
red chillies

1 To make the marinade, pour the lime juice into a large bowl, add the honey, chopped chilli and olive oil and stir until the mixture is well blended and smooth.

2 Cut the chicken breasts into long strips. Add to the marinade and stir gently until thoroughly coated. Cover and chill for at least 1 hour.

3 Thread the chicken on to presoaked wooden skewers and brush with the marinade. Cook under a preheated hot grill or on a barbecue, turning occasionally, until the chicken is cooked, tender and golden brown. Brush the kebabs with more marinade, if necessary, while cooking.

4 Meanwhile, make the avocado sauce. Blend the olive oil and vinegar in a bowl, then beat in the mashed avocado until the mixture is thick and smooth. Stir in the chopped tomato and spring onions, then the soured cream. Garnish the avocado sauce with strips of lime rind. Serve the kebabs with some avocado sauce and garnish with red chilli.

turkey ragoût

Serves 4 – Preparation time: 10 minutes – Cooking time: about 1³/₄ hours

Per serving – Energy: 228 kcals / 954 kJ · Protein: 25 g · Carbohydrate: 7 g · Fat: 6 g · Fibre: 1 g

1	**turkey drumstick,**
	weighing 625 g (1¹/₄ lb)
4	**garlic cloves**
15	**baby onions or shallots**
3	**carrots, diagonally sliced**
300 ml	**(¹/₂ pint) red Burgundy**
	or other full-bodied red wine
	a few thyme sprigs
2	**bay leaves**
2	**tablespoons chopped flat-leaf parsley**
1	**teaspoon port wine jelly**
1	**teaspoon wholegrain mustard**
	salt
	pepper

1 Carefully remove the skin from the turkey drumstick, then make a few slashes in the meat. Finely slice 1 garlic clove into slivers and push them into the slashes. Crush the remaining garlic.

2 Place the drumstick in a large flameproof casserole or roasting tin with the onions, carrots, garlic, red wine, thyme and bay leaves. Season well with salt and pepper. Cover with a lid and cook in a preheated oven at 180°C (350°F), Gas Mark 4 for about 1³/₄ hours.

3 Remove the turkey and vegetables from the casserole and keep hot. Bring the sauce to the boil on the hob, discarding the bay leaves. Add the parsley, port wine jelly and mustard. Boil for 5 minutes until slightly thickened then taste and adjust the seasoning. Carve the turkey and serve with the juices.

alcohol free	
citrus free	✔
dairy free	✔
gluten free	✔
wheat free	✔

herby rabbit casserole

Serves 4 — Preparation time: 10 minutes — Cooking time: about 1 hour

Per serving — Energy: 229 kcals / 962 kJ · Protein: 25 g · Carbohydrate: 15 g · Fat: 5 g · Fibre: 2 g

alcohol free
citrus free
✔ dairy free
gluten free
wheat free

375 g (12 oz) lean rabbit meat, diced
1 tablespoon chopped rosemary,
  plus 4 sprigs, to garnish
1 tablespoon mixed herbs
1 tablespoon plain flour
1 teaspoon olive oil
1 red onion, cut into wedges
1 piece of orange rind
4 sun-dried tomatoes, rehydrated
  and chopped
150 ml (¹/₄ pint) red wine
50 g (2 oz) Puy lentils
sea salt
pepper

1 Place the meat in a large polythene bag. Add the rosemary, mixed herbs and flour and toss well to coat the meat thoroughly.

2 Heat the oil in a large flameproof casserole and fry the meat for a few minutes until browned. Add the onion wedges, orange rind and sun-dried tomatoes.

3 Pour in the wine and add enough water to just cover the meat. Season well. Cover the casserole with a lid and simmer for 45 minutes–1 hour or until the meat is very tender and the vegetables are cooked.

4 Meanwhile, 30 minutes before the end of cooking time, rinse the lentils and cook in a saucepan of boiling water for 20 minutes. Drain and stir into the casserole. Simmer for the remaining 10 minutes. Remove the orange rind before serving and garnish with a rosemary sprig.

ginger chicken with honey

Serves 4 – Preparation time: 15 minutes, plus chilling – Cooking time: 10–15 minutes

Per serving – Energy: 296 kcals / 1240 kJ · Protein: 31 g · Carbohydrate: 19 g · Fat: 11 g · Fibre: 0 g

50 g	**(2 oz) piece of fresh root ginger, peeled and finely chopped**
2	**tablespoons vegetable oil**
3	**boneless, skinless chicken breasts, chopped**
3	**chicken livers, chopped**
1	**onion, finely sliced**
3	**garlic cloves, crushed**
2	**tablespoons dried black fungus (cloud ears), soaked in hot water for 20 minutes**
2	**tablespoons soy sauce**
1	**tablespoon clear honey**
5	**spring onions, chopped**
1	**red chilli, finely sliced into strips, to garnish**
	rice sticks, to serve (optional)

1 Mix the ginger with a little cold water, then drain and squeeze it dry.

2 Heat the oil in a wok and add the chicken breasts and livers. Fry the chicken mixture over a moderate heat for 5 minutes, then remove it with a slotted spoon and set aside.

3 Add the onion to the wok and fry it gently until soft, then add the garlic and the drained mushrooms and stir-fry for 1 minute. Return the chicken mixture to the wok.

4 Stir together the soy sauce and honey in a bowl until blended, then pour this over the chicken and stir well. Add the drained ginger and stir-fry for 2–3 minutes. Finally, add the spring onions. Serve at once, garnished with strips of red chilli and accompanied by rice sticks, if liked.

alcohol free ✔
citrus free ✔
dairy free ✔
gluten free ✔
wheat free ✔

chinese steamed chicken dumplings

Serves 8 – Preparation time: 45 minutes – Cooking time: 20 minutes

Per serving – Energy: 315 kcals / 1333 kJ · Protein: 21 g · Carbohydrate: 52 g · Fat: 3 g · Fibre: 3 g

✔ alcohol free
✔ citrus free
✔ dairy free
  gluten free
  wheat free

500 g **(1 lb) plain flour**
300 ml **(¹/₂ pint) water**
1 **small cabbage, separated into leaves**
    chilli sauce, to serve

Filling:
500 g **(1 lb) boneless, skinless chicken breasts**
250 g **(8 oz) can bamboo shoots,**
    drained and chopped
3 **spring onions, finely chopped**
3 **slices of fresh root ginger,**
    peeled and finely chopped
2 **teaspoons sugar**
2 **teaspoons light soy sauce**
2 **tablespoons dry sherry**
2 **tablespoons chicken stock**
1 **teaspoon sesame oil**
    salt

1 Sift the flour into a large mixing bowl and pour in the water. Mix thoroughly to form a stiff dough. Knead for 5 minutes then place the dough in a bowl, cover with a damp cloth and allow to stand for 10 minutes.

2 Meanwhile, make the filling. Cut the chicken into small bite-sized pieces and place in a bowl with the bamboo shoots, spring onions, ginger, a little salt, the sugar, soy sauce, sherry, stock and sesame oil. Thoroughly mix all the ingredients.

3 Cut the dough in half and form each piece into a long roll. Cut each roll into 16 slices then flatten these into rounds. Roll out to circles, about 7.5 cm (3 inches) in diameter. Place 1 tablespoon of filling in the centre of each circle of dough. Gather up the edges of the dough circles around the filling and twist them at the top to seal it in.

4 Line 1 large or 2 small bamboo steamers with the cabbage leaves. Place the dumplings on the leaves and steam, covered, over a wok of boiling water for 20 minutes. Do not allow the wok to boil dry. Serve hot with chilli sauce.

oriental hot turkey salad

Serves 4 – Preparation time: 15 minutes – Cooking time: 15–20 minutes

Per serving – Energy: 302 kcals / 1265 kJ · Protein: 47 g · Carbohydrate: 2 g · Fat: 12 g · Fibre: 1 g

3	thick lemon grass stalks
25 g	(1 oz) piece of fresh root ginger, peeled and sliced
50 g	(2 oz) butter
1	garlic clove
750 g	(1½ lb) boneless, skinless turkey breast, cut into bite-sized cubes
1	tablespoon dark soy sauce
1	head curly endive
3	spring onions, chopped
1	lemon, cut into wedges, to garnish

1 Cut the lemon grass in half lengthways and then cut the strips in half widthways and mix them with the ginger.

2 Melt the butter in a wok, crush the garlic into it and add the lemon grass and ginger. Cook, stirring continuously, for 2 minutes, then add the turkey and continue stir-frying until the meat has browned all over and is cooked through. Add the soy sauce and cook gently for a few minutes more.

3 Arrange the endive leaves on a serving dish. Sprinkle the spring onions over the endive. Arrange the turkey on top and pour over any juices from the wok. Serve immediately, garnished with the lemon wedges.

alcohol free ✔
citrus free
dairy free
gluten free ✔
wheat free ✔

griddled and roasted guinea fowl joints

Serves 4 – Preparation time: 10 minutes – Cooking time: about 40 minutes

Per serving – Energy: 442 kcals / 1847 kJ · Protein: 46 g · Carbohydrate: 1 g · Fat: 29 g · Fibre: 0 g

1.75 kg	(3½ lb) guinea fowl, cut into 8 pieces
2	tablespoons Dijon mustard
	grated rind and juice of 2 lemons
	vegetable oil, for greasing
	sea salt flakes
	pepper
	griddled butternut squash, to serve

1 Heat a griddle pan or nonstick frying pan, put on the guinea fowl joints and cook for about 6 minutes on each side. The skin should be quite charred, which will give the guinea fowl a good flavour.

2 Mix together the mustard, lemon rind and juice and season with salt and pepper.

3 Remove the guinea fowl from the pan and place in a lightly oiled roasting tin. Using a pastry brush, brush the joints with the mustard mixture, then place on the top shelf of a preheated oven at 200°C (400°F), Gas Mark 6 for 20 minutes. To test if cooked, insert a sharp knife into the thickest part of each joint: the juices should run clear. Serve the guinea fowl with griddled slices of butternut squash.

alcohol free ✔
citrus free
dairy free ✔
gluten free ✔
wheat free ✔

oriental duck with pineapple

Serves 4 – Preparation time: 20 minutes – Cooking time: about 1¹/₄ hours

Per serving – Energy: 448 kcals / 1875 kJ · Protein: 34 g · Carbohydrate: 19 g · Fat: 27 g · Fibre: 3 g

✔ alcohol free
✔ citrus free
✔ dairy free
✔ gluten free
✔ wheat free

2 kg	**(4 lb) skinless, oven-ready duck**
1.2	**litres (2 pints) water**
3	**tablespoons dark soy sauce**
1	**fresh pineapple**
	dash of sesame oil
2	**green chillies, deseeded and thinly sliced**
1	**large garlic clove**
250 g	**(8 oz) can water chestnuts, drained and sliced**
1	**bunch of spring onions, diagonally sliced**

1 Cut the duck in half lengthways, using a meat cleaver and poultry scissors. Place the halves in a wok and pour in the measured water, then add 1 tablespoon of the soy sauce. Put the lid on the wok and bring to the boil. Reduce the heat so that the liquid simmers steadily and cook for 1 hour.

2 While the duck is cooking, prepare the pineapple: trim the leaves off the top and cut off the stalk end. Cut off the peel and cut out all the spines, then slice the fruit in half lengthways and remove the hard core. Cut the pineapple halves into slices and set them aside.

3 Remove the duck from its stock and set aside. Pour the stock out of the wok (this should be chilled and the fat skimmed off, then the stock can be used in another recipe) and wipe out the wok. Oil the wok with a little sesame oil.

4 When the duck is cool enough to handle, cut all the meat off the bones and slice it into pieces. Heat the wok and add the chillies. Crush the garlic into the wok and add the duck. Stir-fry until lightly browned, then add the water chestnuts and pineapple and cook for 1–2 minutes. Stir in the remaining soy sauce and any juice from the fruit, and sprinkle with the spring onions. Cook for 1 minute and serve immediately.

tandoori chicken

Serves 4 – Preparation time: 15 minutes, plus marinating – Cooking time: 20 minutes

Per serving – Energy: 248 kcals / 1040 kJ · Protein: 35 g · Carbohydrate: 7 g · Fat: 9 g · Fibre: 1 g

4 **boneless, skinless chicken breasts**
4 **tablespoons tandoori paste**
   or tandoori powder
2 **onions, sliced**
1 **bunch of coriander, chopped**

To Garnish:
lemon wedges
coriander sprigs

1 Make 3 slashes in the flesh of each chicken breast. Rub the chicken with the tandoori paste or powder and leave to marinate, preferably overnight.

2 Heat a nonstick frying pan. Place the chicken breasts on the pan and cook for 8–10 minutes on each side, allowing a little charred colour to develop.

3 Add the sliced onions and fry until slightly coloured. When the chicken and onions are cooked, mix the onions with the chopped coriander. Serve the chicken with the onion and coriander mixture and garnish with lemon wedges and coriander sprigs.

alcohol free ✔
citrus free
dairy free ✔
gluten free ✔
wheat free ✔

italian lamb with rosemary oil

Serves 4 – Preparation time: 20 minutes – Cooking time: 20–40 minutes

Per serving – Energy: 407 kcals / 1692 kJ · Protein: 39 g · Carbohydrate: 7 g · Fat: 25 g · Fibre: 1 g

2 x **375 g (12 oz) lamb loin or neck fillets,**
   trimmed of fat
4 **garlic cloves, cut into slivers**
   a few small rosemary sprigs
2 **red onions, quartered**
1 **tablespoon chopped rosemary**
4 **tablespoons olive oil**
   sea salt
   pepper

To Serve:
fresh pasta, cooked
Parmesan cheese shavings

1 Make small incisions with a sharp knife all over the fillets and insert the garlic slivers and rosemary sprigs. Heat a nonstick frying pan, put on the fillets, and cook, turning the lamb occasionally, until brown all over, about 20 minutes for rare, or 30–40 minutes for well done meat. Add the onions for the last 10 minutes.

2 Place the chopped rosemary and oil in a mortar and crush with a pestle to release the flavour. Season with salt and pepper. Allow the lamb to rest for 5 minutes before carving into slices. Spoon the rosemary oil over the top and serve at once with the onions. Accompany with fresh pasta and Parmesan shavings.

alcohol free ✔
citrus free ✔
dairy free
gluten free
wheat free

fast chickpea salad

Serves 4 – Preparation time: 10 minutes

Per serving – Energy: 400 kcals / 1678 kJ · Protein: 16 g · Carbohydrate: 35 g · Fat: 23 g · Fibre: 9 g

✔ alcohol free
citrus free
✔ dairy free
gluten free
wheat free

2 x   425 g (14 oz) cans chickpeas
6   spring onions, finely sliced
1   red chilli, deseeded and finely sliced
4   tablespoons chopped parsley
grilled pitta or other warm bread,
to serve (optional)

Dressing:
6   tablespoons extra virgin olive oil
1–2   garlic cloves, crushed
$^1/_2$ teaspoon finely grated lemon rind
3   tablespoons lemon juice
salt
pepper

1 Drain the canned chickpeas into a colander. Rinse them under cold running water, then drain thoroughly. Place them in a large serving bowl with the spring onions, chilli and parsley.

2 Whisk together the dressing ingredients in a small bowl or put them into a screw-topped jar and shake well to combine. Pour the dressing over the salad and toss to mix. Serve the salad with grilled pitta or other warm bread, if liked.

spicy chickpeas

Serves 4 — Preparation time: 15 minutes, plus soaking — Cooking time: about 1¼ hours

Per serving — Energy: 400 kcals / 1684 kJ · Protein: 25 g · Carbohydrate: 48 g · Fat: 13 g · Fibre: 8 g

300 g	(10 oz) dried chickpeas, soaked overnight
1½	teaspoons salt
1	onion, peeled but left whole
6	rindless streaky bacon rashers, chopped
2	onions, chopped
1	garlic clove, crushed
1	red pepper, cored, deseeded and chopped
¼	teaspoon ground black pepper
1	small dried hot red chilli, crumbled
½	teaspoon dried oregano
300 g	(10 oz) tomatoes, skinned and chopped
2	tablespoons tomato purée
	chopped coriander, to garnish

1 Drain the chickpeas and place them in a saucepan with 1 teaspoon of the salt and the whole onion. Cover with cold water, bring to the boil, and boil hard for 10 minutes. Reduce the heat and simmer, uncovered, for about 45 minutes, or until the chickpeas are cooked and tender. Drain and reserve the cooking liquid.

2 Put the bacon in a frying pan and fry until the fat runs. Add the chopped onions, garlic and red pepper and fry until soft. Stir in the remaining salt, the pepper, chilli, oregano, tomatoes, tomato purée and 100 ml (3½ fl oz) of the reserved bean liquid. Add the drained chickpeas and stir well. Simmer for 10 minutes, stirring occasionally. Serve hot, sprinkled with chopped coriander.

alcohol free ✔
citrus free ✔
dairy free ✔
gluten free ✔
wheat free ✔

mixed baked beans

Serves 6 — Preparation time: 15 minutes — Cooking time: 2 hours

Per serving — Energy: 277 kcals / 1177 kJ · Protein: 18 g · Carbohydrate: 52 g · Fat: 1 g · Fibre: 12 g

425 g	(14 oz) can red kidney beans
425 g	(14 oz) can haricot beans
425 g	(14 oz) can aduki beans
250 ml	(8 fl oz) passata (sieved tomatoes)
2	tablespoons molasses
1	teaspoon mustard powder
½	tablespoon Worcestershire sauce or dark soy sauce
½	teaspoon salt
	pinch of ground cloves
1	large onion, finely chopped
2	carrots, diced
2	celery sticks, chopped
2	bay leaves
4	tablespoons chopped parsley
	pepper
	grated Cheddar cheese, to serve (optional)

1 Strain the liquid from the beans and pour half of it into a bowl, discarding the rest. Put the passata, molasses, mustard, Worcestershire or soy sauce, salt and cloves into the liquid and whisk until evenly combined. Season to taste with pepper.

2 Put the beans, the vegetables and bay leaves into a casserole and stir in the spiced liquid. Cover with a tight-fitting lid. Transfer to a preheated oven at 180°C (350°F), Gas Mark 4 and bake for 2 hours. Stir in the parsley and serve in warmed bowls topped with the cheese, if using.

alcohol free ✔
citrus free ✔
dairy free
gluten free ✔
wheat free ✔

mixed bean sauté with almonds and chives

Serves 4 – Preparation time: 30 minutes – Cooking time: 10 minutes
Per serving – Energy: 196 kcals / 815 kJ · Protein: 9 g · Carbohydrate: 10 g · Fat: 14 g · Fibre: 6 g

✔ alcohol free
✔ citrus free
✔ dairy free
✔ gluten free
✔ wheat free

750 g	(1¹/₂ lb) mixed beans (broad beans, runner beans, green beans), trimmed and sliced as necessary
2	tablespoons almond or extra virgin olive oil
1	small leek, trimmed and sliced
2	garlic cloves, sliced
50 g	(2 oz) flaked almonds
2	tablespoons chopped chives
	salt
	pepper

1 Blanch all the beans together in a large saucepan of lightly salted boiling water for 1 minute. Drain, refresh under cold running water and pat dry on kitchen paper.

2 Heat the oil in a large frying pan or wok, add the leek, garlic and almonds and fry gently for 3 minutes until softened. Add the beans, stir-fry for 3–4 minutes until tender and stir in the chives and salt and pepper to taste. Serve immediately.

pumpkin, chickpea and banana curry

Serves 4 – Preparation time: 10–15 minutes – Cooking time: about 45 minutes
Per serving – Energy: 280 kcals / 1173 kJ · Protein: 10 g · Carbohydrate: 30 g · Fat: 15 g · Fibre: 3 g

✔ alcohol free
✔ citrus free
✔ dairy free
✔ gluten free
✔ wheat free

3	tablespoons sunflower oil
1	small onion, sliced
2	garlic cloves, chopped
2	teaspoons grated fresh root ginger
1	teaspoon ground coriander
¹/₂	teaspoon ground cumin
¹/₂	teaspoon turmeric
¹/₄	teaspoon ground cinnamon
625 g	(1¹/₄ lb) pumpkin, peeled, deseeded and cut into cubes
2	tablespoons hot curry paste
2	ripe tomatoes, chopped
2	dried red chillies
300 ml	(¹/₂ pint) vegetable stock
375 g	(12 oz) canned chickpeas, drained
1	large under-ripe banana
1	tablespoon chopped fresh coriander
	plain boiled rice, to serve

1 Heat 2 tablespoons of the oil in a saucepan, add the onion, garlic, ginger and ground spices, and fry over a moderate heat for about 5–6 minutes until the onion is slightly browned.

2 Place the pumpkin in a bowl, add the curry paste and toss well to coat the pumpkin cubes evenly.

3 Add the tomatoes, chillies and stock to the onion mixture, bring to the boil and simmer gently for 15 minutes.

4 Meanwhile, heat the remaining oil in a nonstick frying pan, add the pumpkin and fry for 5 minutes until golden. Add to the onion and tomato sauce with the chickpeas, cover and cook for 20 minutes until the pumpkin is tender.

5 Peel the banana, slice it thickly and stir into the curry 5 minutes before the end of the cooking time. Stir in the chopped coriander and serve immediately with rice.

green lentil and vegetable tagine with couscous

Serves 4 – Preparation time: 20 minutes – Cooking time: 45 minutes

Per serving – Energy: 500 kcals / 2102 kJ · Protein: 17 g · Carbohydrate: 82 g · Fat: 10 g · Fibre: 9 g

125 g	(4 oz) green lentils, rinsed
600 ml	(1 pint) water
4	tablespoons extra virgin olive oil
2	small onions, cut into wedges
2	garlic cloves, chopped
1	tablespoon ground coriander
2	teaspoons ground cumin
1	teaspoon turmeric
1	teaspoon ground cinnamon
12	new potatoes, halved if large
2	large carrots, thickly sliced
250 g	(8 oz) couscous
2	courgettes, sliced
175 g	(6 oz) button mushrooms
300 ml	('/₂ pint) tomato juice
1	tablespoon tomato purée
2	tablespoons chilli sauce, plus extra to serve
125 g	(4 oz) ready-to-eat dried apricots, chopped

1 Put the lentils into a saucepan with the water. Bring to the boil, cover and simmer for 20 minutes.

2 Meanwhile, heat half the oil in a large saucepan and fry the onion, garlic and spices for 5 minutes. Add the potatoes and carrots and fry for a further 5 minutes. Add the lentils with their cooking liquid, cover and simmer gently for 15 minutes.

3 Rinse the couscous under cold running water to moisten all the grains and spread out on a large baking sheet. Sprinkle over a little water then leave to soak for 15 minutes.

4 Heat the remaining oil in a separate pan and fry the courgettes and mushrooms for 4–5 minutes until lightly golden. Add to the lentil mixture with the tomato juice, tomato purée, chilli sauce and dried apricots and return to the boil. Cook for a further 10 minutes until the vegetables and lentils are tender.

5 At the same time steam the couscous for about 6–7 minutes or according to the packet instructions. Transfer the couscous to a large warmed platter, spoon on the vegetable and lentil tagine and serve the juices separately with extra chilli sauce.

alcohol free ✔
citrus free ✔
dairy free ✔
gluten free ✔
wheat free ✔

grilled asparagus salad

Serves 4 – Preparation time: 15 minutes – Cooking time: about 7 minutes

Per serving – Energy: 194 kcals / 798 kJ · Protein: 4 g · Carbohydrate: 5 g · Fat: 18 g · Fibre: 2 g

✔ alcohol free
✔ citrus free
✔ dairy free
✔ gluten free
✔ wheat free

500 g   (1 lb) asparagus
3   tablespoons olive oil
about 50 g (2 oz) rocket
about 50 g (2 oz) lamb's lettuce
2   spring onions, chopped finely
3–4   radishes, thinly sliced
salt
pepper

French Dressing:
3   tablespoons extra virgin olive oil
2   tablespoons white wine vinegar
1   small garlic clove, crushed
pinch caster sugar
1   teaspoon Dijon mustard

To Garnish:
roughly chopped fresh herbs
(tarragon, parsley, chervil, dill)
thin strips of lemon rind

1 Trim the asparagus and, using a vegetable peeler, peel about 5 cm (2 inches) off the bottom of each spear.

2 Arrange the asparagus in a single layer on a baking sheet and brush with olive oil. Cook under a preheated hot grill for about 7 minutes, turning frequently, until the spears are just tender when pierced with the point of a sharp knife and lightly patched with brown. Sprinkle with salt and pepper and leave to cool.

3 Place all the dressing ingredients in a screw-top jar, season to taste and shake vigorously to combine.

4 Arrange the rocket and lamb's lettuce on a serving platter or individual plates. Scatter over the spring onions and radishes. Place the asparagus beside the salad and drizzle with the dressing. Garnish with chopped herbs and strips of lemon rind.

hot leeks, asparagus and peppers with balsamic vinegar

Serves 4 – Preparation time: 10 minutes – Cooking time: 15 minutes

Per serving – Energy: 130 kcals / 536 kJ · Protein: 4 g · Carbohydrate: 8 g · Fat: 9 g · Fibre: 5 g

250 g	(8 oz) baby leeks
250 g	(8 oz) asparagus
2	red peppers, cored, deseeded and quartered
3	tablespoons extra virgin olive oil
2	tablespoons balsamic vinegar
1	bunch of flat-leaf parsley, chopped
	sea salt
	pepper

1 Heat a nonstick frying pan. Place the baby leeks, asparagus and red peppers on the hot pan, in batches, and cook for 5 minutes per batch, turning them occasionally until tender.

2 Put the vegetables into a salad bowl and mix them with the olive oil, balsamic vinegar, chopped parsley, salt and pepper and serve.

alcohol free ✔
citrus free ✔
dairy free ✔
gluten free ✔
wheat free ✔

summer garden salad

Serves 4 – Preparation time: 25 minutes – Cooking time: about 10 minutes

Per serving – Energy: 420 kcals / 1736 kJ · Protein: 8 g · Carbohydrate: 10 g · Fat: 39 g · Fibre: 4 g

1	small cauliflower, broken into florets
175 g	(6 oz) shelled fresh peas (about 375 g/12 oz in the pods)
1	bunch of radishes, trimmed
4	spring onions, chopped
2	tablespoons chopped parsley, plus extra to garnish
	salt
	pepper
	mint sprigs, to garnish

Mint Dressing:

6	tablespoons mayonnaise
3	tablespoons natural yogurt
3	tablespoons water
$^1/_2$	garlic clove, crushed
12	tablespoons finely chopped mint

1 Bring a saucepan of water to the boil and add the cauliflower florets. When the water returns to the boil, cook the florets for about 3 minutes, until just tender. Drain the florets in a colander, reserving the cooking water, and refresh under cold running water, then drain thoroughly.

2 Add the peas to the saucepan of cauliflower cooking water. Cook for 4 minutes then drain, refresh and cool as for the cauliflower.

3 Combine the cauliflower, peas, radishes and spring onions in a serving bowl. Add the parsley, with salt and pepper to taste.

4 To make the dressing, stir all the ingredients together in a small bowl. Taste and adjust the seasoning. Drizzle the dressing over the salad just before serving and toss lightly. Garnish with mint sprigs and chopped parsley.

alcohol free ✔
citrus free ✔
dairy free
gluten free ✔
wheat free ✔

warm butternut squash and sunshine salad

Serves 4 – Preparation time: 20 minutes – Cooking time: about 40 minutes

Per serving – Energy: 250 kcals / 1039 kJ · Protein: 5 g · Carbohydrate: 12 g · Fat: 21 g · Fibre: 2 g

✔ alcohol free
✔ citrus free
✔ dairy free
✔ gluten free
✔ wheat free

1	small butternut squash, halved, deseeded and cut into 2.5 cm (1 inch) wedges
175 g	(6 oz) baby sweetcorn cobs
2	yellow courgettes, cut diagonally into 1 cm ($^1/_2$ inch) pieces
50 g	(2 oz) toasted pine nuts
1	bunch of oregano, chopped
4	tablespoons lemon-infused olive oil
	sea salt flakes
	pepper

1 Heat a nonstick frying pan, add the butternut squash in batches and cook until soft, about 6 minutes on each side. To test, insert the tip of a knife into the thickest part of the squash: it should go in easily. Arrange the cooked squash on a warmed serving dish.

2 Add the sweetcorn cobs to the pan and cook for 6 minutes, constantly moving them until they are lightly browned. Arrange on the same dish as the pumpkin. Add the courgette pieces and cook for 2 minutes on each side, then add to the other vegetables.

3 Sprinkle the pine nuts, oregano and salt and pepper over the salad then drizzle with the lemon oil and serve.

warm mixed vegetable salad with basil dressing

Serves 4 – Preparation time: 15 minutes – Cooking time: 30 minutes

Per serving – Energy: 208 kcals / 860 kJ · Protein: 3 g · Carbohydrate: 11 g · Fat: 17 g · Fibre: 4 g

✔ alcohol free
✔ citrus free
✔ dairy free
✔ gluten free
✔ wheat free

2	red peppers
1	red onion, cut in 1 cm ($^1/_2$ inch) slices
1	aubergine, cut in 1 cm ($^1/_2$ inch) slices
2	courgettes, cut diagonally in 1 cm ($^1/_2$ cm) slices
	sea salt flakes
	pepper
	basil leaves, to garnish

Dressing:

1	large bunch of basil, finely chopped
1	garlic clove, crushed
6	tablespoons olive oil
2	tablespoons white wine vinegar

1 Slice the stalk end off each pepper, then slice down to give 4–5 flat, wide slices, leaving the seeds still attached to the core. Discard the core.

2 Heat a griddle pan or nonstick frying pan and cook the onions for 3 minutes on each side, the peppers for 4 minutes on each side, the aubergine for 3 minutes on each side and the courgettes for 2 minutes on each side. Arrange the cooked vegetables on a large platter.

3 To make the dressing, place all the ingredients in a screw-top jar and shake well to combine thoroughly. Season the cooked vegetables, drizzle over the basil dressing and garnish with basil leaves. Serve warm.

bean salad with griddled onion

Serves 4 – Preparation time: 20 minutes – Cooking time: 20 minutes

Per serving – Energy: 524 kcals / 2192 kJ · Protein: 19 g · Carbohydrate: 50 g · Fat: 29 g · Fibre: 8 g

3	**red or mild white onions, cut into wedges but root ends left intact**
500 g	**(1 lb) canned cannellini beans, drained and rinsed**
	flat-leaf parsley, to garnish

Dressing:

150 ml	**(¹/₄ pint) olive oil**
5	**tablespoons lemon juice**
2	**garlic cloves, crushed**
2	**tablespoons finely chopped flat-leaf parsley**
	pinch of English mustard powder
	pinch of sugar
	salt
	pepper

1 Heat a griddle pan or nonstick frying pan. Place the onions on the hot pan and cook for about 4 minutes on each side, or until they are charred. If they are charring too much, reduce the heat. Remove from the heat and allow the onions to cool on a board.

2 To make the dressing, put all the ingredients into a screw-top jar and shake well.

3 Place the onions in a large bowl, pour on the dressing and mix in the beans. Heap on a serving dish and garnish with some torn parsley.

alcohol free ✔
citrus free
dairy free ✔
gluten free ✔
wheat free ✔

baby vegetable stir-fry with orange and oyster sauce

Serves 4 – Preparation time: 12 minutes – Cooking time: 12–15 minutes

Per serving – Energy: 148 kcals / 620 kJ · Protein: 3 g · Carbohydrate: 22 g · Fat: 6 g · Fibre: 2 g

✔ alcohol free
citrus free
✔ dairy free
✔ gluten free
✔ wheat free

2	tablespoons olive or walnut oil
175 g	(6 oz) baby carrots
175 g	(6 oz) baby sweetcorn cobs
175 g	(6 oz) small button mushrooms
	pepper

Orange and Oyster Sauce:

2	tablespoons cornflour
4	tablespoons water
	finely grated rind and juice of 1 large orange
2	tablespoons oyster sauce
1	tablespoon dry sherry vinegar

1 To make the sauce, blend the cornflour in a jug with the water then add the orange rind and juice, oyster sauce and sherry vinegar. Stir well to combine.

2 Heat a wok until hot. Add the oil and heat over a moderate heat until hot but not smoking. Add the carrots and sweetcorn and stir-fry for 5 minutes, then add the mushrooms and stir-fry for 3–4 minutes.

3 Pour in the sauce mixture and bring to the boil over a high heat, stirring constantly until thickened and glossy. Add pepper to taste, garnish with parsley and serve.

stir-fried vegetables

Serves 3 – Preparation time: 10 minutes, plus soaking – Cooking time: 3–4 minutes

Per serving – Energy: 195 kcals / 804 kJ · Protein: 5 g · Carbohydrate: 11 g · Fat: 15 g · Fibre: 3 g

✔ alcohol free
✔ citrus free
✔ dairy free
✔ gluten free
✔ wheat free

5–6	dried shiitake mushrooms or 50 g (2 oz) button mushrooms
250 g	(8 oz) Chinese leaves
175 g	(6 oz) carrots
125 g	(4 oz) green beans, trimmed
4	tablespoons vegetable oil
1	teaspoon salt
1	teaspoon sugar
1	tablespoon light soy sauce

1 Put the dried shiitake mushrooms into a bowl, pour over some warm water, then cover and leave to soak for 25–30 minutes. Drain the mushrooms and squeeze dry. Discard the hard stalks and finely slice the mushrooms. If using fresh mushrooms, just wipe and slice them.

2 Cut the Chinese leaves and carrots diagonally into thin slices. If the green beans are small, leave them whole; if they are long, cut them in half.

3 Heat the oil in a wok, add the Chinese leaves and carrots and stir-fry briskly for 30 seconds. Add the beans and mushrooms and continue stir-frying for another 30 seconds. Add the salt and sugar, then toss the vegetables until well mixed. Stir in the soy sauce and cook for 1 further minute. Transfer to a warmed serving dish and serve immediately.

stir-fried spiced cucumber

Serves 4 – Preparation time: 10 minutes, plus draining – Cooking time: 5 minutes

Per serving – Energy: 49 kcals / 200 kJ · Protein: 1 g · Carbohydrate: 3 g · Fat: 4 g · Fibre: 31 g

1½	cucumbers, peeled
2	teaspoons salt
1	tablespoon oil
¼	teaspoon chilli bean sauce or chilli powder
6	garlic cloves, crushed
1½	tablespoons black beans, roughly chopped
5	tablespoons chicken stock
1	teaspoon sesame oil cucumber slices, to garnish

1 Slice the cucumbers in half lengthways, remove the seeds and cut the flesh into 2.5 cm (1 inch) cubes. Sprinkle them with the salt and leave to drain in a colander for about 30 minutes. Rinse in cold running water, drain well and dry thoroughly on kitchen paper.

2 Heat the oil in a wok, then add the chilli bean sauce or chilli powder, garlic and black beans and stir-fry for about 30 seconds. Add the cucumber and toss well to coat the cubes with the spices. Pour in the stock and continue stir-frying over a high heat for 3–4 minutes, until almost all the liquid has evaporated and the cucumber is tender.

3 Transfer to 4 warmed serving dishes. Sprinkle with sesame oil, garnish with slices of raw cucumber and serve immediately.

alcohol free ✔
citrus free ✔
dairy free ✔
gluten free ✔
wheat free ✔

mexican christmas eve salad

Serves 4 – Preparation time: 25 minutes

Per serving – Energy: 392 kcals / 1636 kJ · Protein: 8 g · Carbohydrate: 35 g · Fat: 26 g · Fibre: 7 g

1	green apple, cored and sliced
2	oranges, segmented
½	fresh pineapple, peeled, cored and sliced
1	large banana, sliced
1	large red apple, cored and sliced
125 ml	(4 fl oz) lemon juice
1	large lettuce, separated into leaves
2	small cooked beetroots, peeled and diced

Dressing:

6	tablespoons olive oil
2	tablespoons lemon juice
1	teaspoon sugar
¼	teaspoon salt

To Garnish:

75 g	(3 oz) unsalted roasted peanuts
1	tablespoon chopped parsley

1 Prepare all the fruits and sprinkle with lemon juice to prevent discoloration.

2 To make the dressing, put all the ingredients into a screw-top jar and shake vigorously until the sugar has dissolved.

3 Arrange the lettuce, beetroot and fruit on a plate and sprinkle the dressing over the salad. Garnish with the peanuts and parsley and serve immediately.

alcohol free ✔
citrus free
dairy free ✔
gluten free ✔
wheat free ✔

vegetable fajitas

Serves 4 – Preparation time: 15 minutes – Cooking time: 15–20 minutes

Per serving – Energy: 377 kcals / 1590 kJ · Protein: 11 g · Carbohydrate: 71 g · Fat: 8 g · Fibre: 9 g

✔ alcohol free
✔ citrus free
✔ dairy free
  gluten free
  wheat free

2	**tablespoons olive oil**
2	**large onions, thinly sliced**
2	**garlic cloves, crushed**
2	**red peppers, cored, deseeded and thinly sliced**
2	**green peppers, cored, deseeded and thinly sliced**
4	**green chillies, deseeded and thinly sliced**
2	**teaspoons chopped oregano**
250 g	**(8 oz) button mushrooms, sliced**
	salt
	pepper
	To Serve:
12	**warmed tortillas**
	chives

1 Heat the olive oil in a large frying pan and gently sauté the onions and garlic for about 5 minutes until they are soft and golden brown.

2 Add the red and green peppers, chillies and oregano and stir well. Sauté for about 10 minutes, until cooked and tender.

3 Add the button mushrooms and cook quickly for 1 minute, stirring to mix the mushrooms thoroughly with the other vegetables. Season the vegetable mixture with salt and pepper to taste.

4 To serve, spoon the hot vegetable mixture into the warmed tortillas and roll up or fold over. Serve hot, garnished with chives.

marinated mushroom salad with straw potatoes

Serves 4 – Preparation time: 15 minutes, plus marinating – Cooking time: 2–3 minutes

Per serving – Energy: 427 kcals / 1765 kJ · Protein: 5 g · Carbohydrate: 13 g · Fat: 40 g · Fibre: 4 g

500 g	(1 lb) mushrooms, very thinly sliced
	vegetable oil, for frying
250 g	(8 oz) potatoes,
	cut into very thin matchsticks
125 g	(4 oz) salad leaves
6	spring onions, thinly sliced

Balsamic Dressing:

2	teaspoons balsamic vinegar
2	teaspoons wholegrain mustard
5	tablespoons extra virgin olive oil
	salt
	pepper

1 Place the mushrooms on a large plate. Whisk together the dressing ingredients and pour half of the dressing over the mushrooms. Set aside for 1 hour, turning occasionally until softened.

2 Heat 1 cm (½ inch) of oil in a frying pan and fry the potato straws for 2–3 minutes until crisp and golden. Drain on kitchen paper.

3 Toss the salad leaves with the remaining dressing, then arrange them on serving plates. Put the marinated mushrooms on the salad leaves and top with the spring onions and straw potatoes. Serve at once.

alcohol free ✔
citrus free ✔
dairy free ✔
gluten free ✔
wheat free ✔

flageolet bean and roasted vegetable salad

Serves 4 – Preparation time: 20 minutes, plus cooling – Cooking time: 40 minutes

Per serving – Energy: 307 kcals / 1283 kJ · Protein: 9 g · Carbohydrate: 23 g · Fat: 21 g · Fibre: 4 g

1	aubergine, stalk removed
1	red pepper, halved, cored and deseeded
1	yellow pepper, halved, cored
	and deseeded
1	courgette, topped and tailed
4	garlic cloves, peeled but left whole
4	tablespoons olive oil
1	teaspoon coarse sea salt
300 g	(10 oz) canned flageolet beans
2	tablespoons chopped mixed herbs
	(parsley and oregano; or coriander
	and mint)
1	quantity French Dressing
	(see page 104)
	pepper

1 Cut all the vegetables into strips and put them into a roasting tin. Add the garlic. Sprinkle over the oil, sea salt and pepper. Place in a preheated oven at 200°C (400°F), Gas Mark 6 and roast for 40 minutes. Transfer to a shallow bowl and leave to cool.

2 Add the beans and toss lightly. Stir the herbs into the French dressing, pour over the salad and serve.

alcohol free ✔
citrus free ✔
dairy free ✔
gluten free ✔
wheat free ✔

griddled polenta with field mushrooms

Serves 4 — Preparation time: 35 minutes, plus cooling — Cooking time: 20 minutes

Per serving — Energy: 650 kcals / 2704 kJ · Protein: 32 g · Carbohydrate: 47 g · Fat: 36 g · Fibre: 2 g

alcohol free

✔ citrus free

dairy free

✔ gluten free

✔ wheat free

1	litre (1¾ pints) boiling water
250 g	(8 oz) instant polenta flour
1	tablespoon olive oil
50 g	(2 oz) butter
375 g	(12 oz) field mushrooms, sliced
2	garlic cloves, crushed
1	bunch of thyme, chopped
2	tablespoons white wine
250 g	(8 oz) Parmesan cheese, shaved into slivers
	sea salt flakes
	pepper

1 Bring the water to the boil in a large saucepan, pour in the polenta, season with salt and pepper and mix well until smooth. Turn the heat down and continue to mix for about 5 minutes until the polenta thickens and the water has been absorbed. The mixture will become very thick and hard to work. Using a spatula, spread the polenta on a chopping board, or in an oiled 23 cm (9 inch) springform cake tin. Leave to cool for about 1 hour.

2 Heat the oil and butter in a small saucepan, add the mushrooms, garlic and thyme and cook for 8 minutes, until soft and dark. Add the white wine and simmer for 2 minutes, then season with salt and pepper. Remove the pan from the heat and keep warm.

3 Heat a griddle pan or nonstick frying pan, cut the polenta into slices or wedges and griddle for about 4 minutes on each side. Serve the griddled polenta with the mushrooms and sprinkled with Parmesan.

long fusilli with asparagus, peas and lemon

Serves 4 – Preparation time: 15 minutes – Cooking time: about 15 minutes

Per serving – Energy: 913 kcals / 3823 kJ · Protein: 52 g · Carbohydrate: 77 g · Fat: 46 g · Fibre: 3 g

250 g (8 oz) dried long fusilli
375 g (12 oz) asparagus spears, trimmed
          and cut into 5 cm (2 inch) lengths
125 g (4 oz) shelled fresh peas,
          (250 g/8 oz in the pods)
    2 large tomatoes, skinned, deseeded
          and chopped
          small handful of basil leaves, torn
          small handful of parsley leaves, torn
          rind and juice of 1 small lemon
    1 quantity French Dressing
          (see page 104)
          salt
          pepper

1 Bring a large saucepan of water to the boil, add the pasta and cook according to packet instructions until just tender. Drain in a colander and rinse under cold running water. Drain thoroughly and transfer to a serving bowl.

2 Cook the asparagus in a shallow saucepan of boiling water for 4–5 minutes, until almost tender. Drain in a colander, cool under cold running water, then drain thoroughly.

3 Add the asparagus, peas, tomatoes, basil, parsley and lemon rind to the pasta and season well with salt and pepper. Just before serving add the lemon juice to the salad with the French dressing. Toss lightly.

alcohol free ✔
citrus free
dairy free ✔
gluten free ✔
wheat free ✔

rocket risotto

Serves 4 – Preparation time: 5 minutes – Cooking time: 25 minutes

Per serving – Energy: 289 kcals / 1209 kJ · Protein: 7 g · Carbohydrate: 58 g · Fat: 2 g · Fibre: 0 g

    1 teaspoon olive oil
    1 onion, finely chopped
300 g (10 oz) arborio rice
  1.2 litres (2 pints) hot vegetable stock
  50 g (2 oz) rocket leaves
          salt
          pepper

1 Heat the oil in a nonstick frying pan, add the onion and fry for a few minutes until softened.

2 Add the rice to the pan, stirring well to coat the grains with the oil, then pour in enough hot stock to cover the rice. Stir the rice frequently and simmer gently, gradually adding the remaining stock as each ladleful is absorbed by the rice. Test the rice after 18 minutes and, if it is not done, cook for a little longer, still stirring so that it does not stick on the bottom of the pan.

3 Stir in the rocket, reserving 4 leaves to garnish, and cook just until the leaves start to wilt. Season to taste and serve each portion garnished with a rocket leaf.

alcohol free ✔
citrus free ✔
dairy free ✔
gluten free ✔
wheat free ✔

griddled vegetable risotto

Serves 4 – Preparation time: 10 minutes – Cooking time: 30 minutes

Per serving – Energy: 727 kcals / 3039 kJ · Protein: 20 g · Carbohydrate: 73 g · Fat: 40 g · Fibre: 3 g

alcohol free
✔ citrus free
dairy free
✔ gluten free
✔ wheat free

1	**red onion, sliced**
125 g	**(4 oz) asparagus, chopped**
2	**courgettes, sliced**
4	**mushrooms, sliced**
125 g	**(4 oz) butternut squash, peeled and diced**
1	**tablespoon olive oil**
125 g	**(4 oz) butter**
1	**garlic clove, crushed**
1	**onion, finely chopped**
300 g	**(10 oz) arborio rice**
1	**litre (1³/₄ pints) hot vegetable or chicken stock**
75 ml	**(3 fl oz) dry white wine**
1	**tablespoon chopped sage**
125 g	**(4 oz) Parmesan cheese, grated**

To Garnish:
1 tablespoon chopped sage
Parmesan cheese shavings

1 Heat a griddle pan or nonstick frying pan and griddle all the vegetables, in batches, until tender, cooking each one for about 5 minutes.

2 Meanwhile, make the risotto. Heat the oil and half the butter in a heavy-based saucepan, add the garlic and onion and cook for 2 minutes. Do not allow to brown.

3 Add the rice to the pan, stirring well to coat the grains with the butter mixture, then pour in enough hot stock to cover the rice. Stir the rice frequently and simmer gently, gradually adding the remaining stock as each ladleful is absorbed by the rice. Test the rice after 18 minutes and, if it is not done, cook for a little longer, still stirring so that it does not stick on the bottom of the pan.

4 Add the white wine, sage, grated Parmesan, griddled vegetables and the remaining butter. Mix well and cook for 3 minutes; it should have a creamy texture. Serve, garnished with chopped sage and Parmesan shavings.

pasta with roasted tomatoes and basil

Serves 4 – Preparation time: 25 minutes – Cooking time: about 45 minutes

Per serving – Energy: 468 kcals / 1952 kJ · Protein: 12 g · Carbohydrate: 72 g · Fat: 15 g · Fibre: 2 g

20	cherry tomatoes
8	garlic cloves, peeled but left whole
1	tablespoon chopped thyme
375 g	(12 oz) dried tagliatelle
	or pasta bows (farfalle)
1	tablespoon olive oil
16	black olives, pitted
	handful of shredded basil leaves
1	quantity French Dressing (see page 104), excluding garlic
	sea salt
	pepper

alcohol free ✔
citrus free ✔
dairy free ✔
gluten free
wheat free

1 Halve the tomatoes. Arrange them, cut-side up, on a baking sheet. Tuck the garlic cloves among them and sprinkle with the thyme and 2 teaspoons salt. Season generously with pepper and roast in a preheated oven at 190°C (375°F), Gas Mark 5 for 45 minutes, until the tomatoes are soft and wrinkled and have lost much of their moisture. Leave to cool. Remove the garlic cloves and set aside in a small bowl; mash lightly.

2 Meanwhile, bring a large saucepan of water to the boil, add the pasta and cook according to the packet instructions, until just tender. Drain in a colander and rinse under cold running water. Drain thoroughly and place in a large bowl. Add the olive oil and toss well.

3 Add the cooled roasted tomatoes to the pasta with the olives and basil. Stir the dressing into the mashed garlic, mix well and pour over the salad. Toss lightly and serve.

mixed onion tagliatelle with pecorino

Serves 4 – Preparation time: 20 minutes – Cooking time: 30 minutes

Per serving – Energy: 760 kcals / 3210 kJ · Protein: 29 g · Carbohydrate: 90 g · Fat: 36 g · Fibre: 4 g

✔ alcohol free
✔ citrus free
  dairy free
  gluten free
  wheat free

4	**small leeks, cut into large chunks**
4	**spring onions**
2	**red onions, cut into wedges, with root ends left intact**
1	**white onion, cut into wedges, with root ends left intact**
2	**shallots, cut into wedges, with root ends left intact**
4	**garlic cloves, sliced**
500 g	**(1 lb) fresh tagliatelle**
150 ml	**(¼ pint) double cream**
175 g	**(6 oz) pecorino cheese, coarsely grated**
1	**handful of chives, snipped**
	sea salt flakes
	pepper

1 Heat a nonstick frying pan, add the leeks and cook over a low heat for 6 minutes, turning constantly. Transfer to a shallow baking dish and place in a preheated oven at 180°C (350°F), Gas Mark 4 to continue to soften. Repeat the process with the spring onions, cooking them for 4 minutes, then add to the leeks in the oven.

2 Cook the onions and shallots in the pan for 3–6 minutes, depending on size, then transfer to the oven with the leeks and spring onions. Quickly fry the garlic slices for 1 minute on each side, then remove them and set aside. Continue to cook the onion mixture in the oven for a further 10 minutes.

3 Meanwhile, heat a large saucepan of boiling water, stir in the pasta and cook according to packet instructions, or until tender. Drain well, then return to the pan. Add the onion mixture, garlic, cream, pecorino and chives. Season with salt and pepper. Toss well and serve.

griddled figs with greek yogurt and honey

Serves 4 – Preparation time: 5 minutes – Cooking time: 10 minutes

Per serving – Energy: 404 kcals / 1687 kJ · Protein: 19 g · Carbohydrate: 27 g · Fat: 25 g · Fibre: 3 g

8	**ripe figs**
4	**tablespoons Greek yogurt**
2	**tablespoons clear honey**

1 Heat a griddle pan or non-stick frying pan and add the figs. Cook for 8 minutes, turning occasionally, until they are charred on the outside. Remove and cut in half. Arrange the figs on 4 plates and serve with a spoonful of yogurt and some honey spooned over the top.

alcohol free ✔
citrus free ✔
dairy free
gluten free ✔
wheat free ✔

melon and rosewater salad

Serves 4 – Preparation time: 15 minutes – Cooking time: 1 hour

Per serving – Energy: 106 kcals / 450 kJ · Protein: 3 g · Carbohydrate: 20 g · Fat: 2 g · Fibre: 4 g

2	**small galia melons**
1	**mango**
1	**papaya**
2	**tablespoons lime juice**
4	**tablespoons rosewater**
1	**tablespoon chopped lemon zest**
1	**tablespoon pistachio nuts**

1 Cut the melons in half lengthways. Holding the melons over a sieve set over a large bowl – to catch all the juices – scoop out and discard the melon seeds. Using a melon baller, scoop out the flesh and place in the bowl with the melon juice.

2 Cut the mango down each side of the central stone. Peel and cut the flesh into small cubes. Halve the papaya, scoop out and discard the seeds, then peel and dice the flesh. Add the mango and papaya to the melon balls in the bowl.

3 Mix the lime juice and rosewater together, and pour over the fruit. Chill in the refrigerator for 1 hour. Stir in the lemon zest and spoon the fruit mixture into a serving bowl. Sprinkle with the nuts and serve.

alcohol free ✔
citrus free
dairy free ✔
gluten free ✔
wheat free ✔

glossary

ALLERGEN: Food or substance that triggers an allergic reaction.

ALLERGIC REACTION: Reaction caused by immune reaction to an allergen. Symptoms may include joint pains, swelling, sneezing and mucus production.

ALLERGY: Immune reaction to food or other substance. Common allergies include eczema, asthma and hay fever.

ANALGESICS: Painkillers.

ANKYLOSING: Causing stiffness.

ARTHRITIS: Inflammatory condition of the joints.

ARTHROGRAPHY: An X-ray in which dye is injected into the joint so it can be seen clearly.

ARTHROSCOPY: Diagnostic test in which a tiny telescope is used to examine the inside of the joint.

AUTO-IMMUNE DISEASE: Any condition in which the body's immune system turns against itself.

CARTILAGE: Strong, shock-absorbing layer of tissue on the end of bones, which helps the bone ends to move smoothly.

CORTICOSTEROIDS: A type of anti-inflammatory drug – it is commonly known as steroids.

DISEASE-MODIFYING ANTI-RHEUMATIC DRUGS (DMARDS): Drugs used primarily in rheumatoid arthritis to reduce symptoms such as pain and stiffness. They may sometimes halt the progress of rheumatoid arthritis.

FIBROMYALGIA: A type of rheumatism which causes pain and tenderness in the muscles and ligaments.

IMMUNE SYSTEM: The body's natural defence mechanism.

IMMUNE COMPLEXES: Molecules which provoke inflammation, found in some cases of rheumatoid arthritis and other forms of inflammatory arthritis.

INFLAMMATION: An immune reaction involving pain, swelling and redness caused by the release of inflammatory chemicals.

JOINT CAPSULE: The tough, fibrous ball of ligaments around a joint.

LIGAMENTS: Tough fibrous bands attached to bones on either side of a joint to keep the joint stable.

NSAIDS (NON-STEROIDAL ANTI-INFLAMMATORY DRUGS): Drugs used to reduce inflammation and quell pain and swelling.

POLYMYALGIA RHEUMATICA (PMR): A rheumatic disease affecting a large number of muscles in the body.

RHEUMATISM: Aches and pains in the muscles and soft tissues.

RHEUMATOID FACTOR: An antibody found in some people with rheumatoid arthritis and SLE.

SPONDYLOSIS: Osteoarthritis of the small joints in the neck and back.

SYNOVIUM: Membrane lining the joint capsule. It produces synovial fluid.

SYNOVIAL FLUID: A clear, lubricating fluid produced by the synovium, which nourishes the joint and helps cartilage remain slippery.

TENDONS: Strong fibrous cords that attach muscles to bones.

URIC ACID: A natural breakdown product of protein found in the urine. High levels are found in gout sufferers.

bibliography

ARTHRITIS AND RHEUMATISM

Maximising the Arthritis Cure, Theodosakis, Jason, Brenda Adderly and Barry Fox, Century, London, 1997

Diet and Arthritis, Darlington,Dr Gail and Linda Gamlin, Vermillion, London, 1998

Arthritis, The Complete Guide to Relief, Sobel, Dava & Arthur C Klein, Robinson, London, 1998

Mayo Clinic on Arthritis, Mayo Clinic, Boston, 1999

Curing Arthritis the Drug-free Way, Hills, Margaret, Sheldon Press, London, 1994

Recipes for Health, Arthritis,Chaitow, Alkmini and Leon Chaitow, Thorsons, London, 1996

COMPLEMENTARY MEDICINE

The Hamlyn Encyclopedia of Complementary Health, Edited by Nikki Bradford, Hamlyn, London, 1996

FOOD

Body Foods for Women, Clarke, Jane, Weidenfeld & Nicholson, London, 1997

Foods that Harm, Foods that Heal, Reader's Digest, London, 1996

The Optimum Nutrition Bible, Holford, Patrick, Piatkus, London, 1997

useful addresses

Arthritis Care
18 Stephenson Way, London NW1 2HD
Tel: 0808 8004050 or 020 79161500

Arthritis Research Campaign
Copeman House, St Mary's Court, St Mary's Gate, Chesterfield, Derbyshire S41 7TD
Tel: 01246 558033

ACUPUNCTURE

British Acupuncture Council
63 Jeddo Road, London W12 9HQ
Tel: 020 8735 0400

AROMATHERAPY

Aromatherapy Organisations Council
PO Box 19834, London SE25 6WF
Tel: 020 8251 7912

AYURVEDIC MEDICINE

Ayurvedic Medical Association UK
c/o The Hale Clinic, 7 Park Crescent, London W1N 3HE
Tel: 020 7631 0156

CHINESE MEDICINE

Register of Chinese Herbal Medicine
PO Box 400, Wembley, Middlesex HA9 9NZ
Tel: 020 7470 8740

WESTERN HERBALISM

National Institute of Medical Herbalists
56 Longbrooke Street, Exeter, EX4 6AH
Tel: 01392 426022

HOMOEOPATHY

The Society of Homoeopaths
4a Artizan Road, Northampton NN1 4HU
Tel: 01604 621400

OSTEOPATHY

British School of Osteopathy
275 Borough High Street, London SE1 1JE
Tel: 020 74070222

COMPLEMENTARY MEDICINE

Institute of Complementary Medicine
PO Box 194, London SE16 7QZ
Tel: 020 7237 5165

index